GOAL-POST

www.victorianfootball.co.uk

Goal-Post

VICTORIAN FOOTBALL

Edited by Paul Brown

Published in 2012 by Goal-Post
An imprint of Superelastic Books

ISBN-13:
9780956227034

A CIP data record for this book is
available from the British Library.

The materials included in this collection were
originally published between 1862 and 1900.
Every effort has been made to identify rights
holders and obtain permissions where relevant.
The publisher will be pleased to rectify any
omissions at the earliest opportunity.

Cover image from Sketches at the International
Football Match by William Ralston, 1872.

www.victorianfootball.co.uk

Contents

~

*"Success to football,
irrespective of class or creed."*

Introduction

~

WELCOME to Goal-Post, a Victorian football anthology. This is a dip of a toe into the broad waters of 19th century football writing. It's a collection of contemporary newspaper and periodical articles and book extracts featuring some of the players, officials, clubs and matches that helped shape and define the game.

It's easy to get lost in the Victorian football archives, drawn into the boxes and binders and microfiches by colourful, first-hand accounts of the beginnings of the greatest game in the world. These writers were covering something that was fresh and new, and their enthusiasm is apparent on the page. Although football coverage was initially sparse, there was a rapidly-growing appetite to watch, learn and play, and newspapers and periodicals played an important role in promoting and developing the game.

By the end of the 19th century there were more than 250 daily and evening newspapers in Britain, and many of them had worked out that covering the popular game increased readership. As a result, the wealth of football material in the archives is huge. Despite the best efforts of our library services, these archives are not easily accessible to the general reader. A great many valuable, informative and entertaining pieces of football writing are hidden away, never to be seen by the modern football fan. Goal-Post seeks to make a representative selection of this writing accessible and available to all.

Although football was played throughout the Victorian era, this collection concentrates on the latter half of the period, and the development of association football. Only one of the pieces in this collection pre-dates the formation of the Football Association in 1863, and George Forrest's attempt to set out a clear set of rules for the game highlights why there was pressing need for such an organisation to be created. Earlier forms of football are covered, however, and Montague Shearman's important history of football explains how the game developed from "beastlie furie" to codification, via public schools and northern towns. There is also an account of the first ever association football match, an unusual fourteen-a-side affair. Subsequent match reports included here demonstrate how the game developed in format and style, and in another piece C. W. Alcock provides an insight into early football tactics. It's also interesting to note the development of the spectator, from curious bystander to full-throated football fan, bellowing songs and cheers from increasingly-crowded touchlines.

What especially delights here are the details, such as those afforded to the great spectacle of the 1888 FA Cup Final at the Oval. The steady stream of cabs and movements of the telegraph boys, the crowd bursting into song – 20,000 voices singing Two Lovely Black Eyes and Rule Britannia – and then the emergence of the players, with their whalebone pads "in case of a chance hack", and the referee and umpires "each armed with a little flag and a whistle".

Also fascinating is a comparison between the two interviews with England captains included here. In 1888, Tinsley Lindley discusses a probable split between amateurs and professionals. By 1896, G. O. Smith, an amateur himself, has embraced professionalism as a means to move the game forward. Smith is much more concerned with the apparent scourge of "funking" in football. "In my opinion it is impossible of cure," he says. "A boy if he 'funks' will probably go on 'funking' when he becomes bigger."

There is a revealing interview with Tottenham secretary/manager Frank Brettell, who plans to turn the newly-professional Hotspurs into a big club with a then-huge budget of £8,000 and "many real live First League players". Henry Leach's fascinating account of life as a travelling football reporter highlights some of the "discomforts of the business", and the myriad difficulties involved with transporting a team of footballers around the country. Other pieces provide further insight into the running of a Victorian club, from getting overindulged players back into shape during pre-season training to dealing with the "monstrously rude" public reaction to lost matches and other "misfortunes". "If our famous left winger happens to be seen in the street the worse for beer," a committee member writes, "this is held to be the fault of the committee, and not of the left winger himself."

Those who have grown weary of certain aspects of modern football will no doubt find much to admire in the Victorian game. Commercialisation has yet to take hold, and the primary motive for playing and watching football remains pure enjoyment. However, these pages also provide tales of overpaid players, cheating, violence, legal battles and general bad behaviour. It's possible to conclude that football hasn't really changed that much in the 150 years between the writing of the earliest of these pieces and their publication in these pages.

While the work of these Victorian football writers can be brought to the attention of the modern reader, not all of the writers can be identified. Many wrote anonymously, either uncredited or behind nom de plumes. For every Henry Leach or Helen Zimmern there is a "Crude Critic" or "Spectator". Brief biographical details are provided for those writers who can be identified. Other footnotes and commentary have been kept to a minimum in order to allow the pieces to stand on their own merits. Some edits have been made for length, and, where noted, certain pieces have been amalgamated from more than one source. Otherwise, the pieces are presented here as they were originally published.

The aim of Goal-Post is not to provide a history lesson, but to offer a flavour, an insight into what it must have been like to have enjoyed football in the latter part of the Victorian era. It's hoped that the pieces selected for this volume will provide a representative overview of football writing in the game's formative years. There is plenty more where this collection came from, and it is intended that this will be the first of several volumes. Interested parties are urged to visit the website www.victorianfootball.co.uk.

All that remains is to raise a toast, as was raised after the very first association football match in 1864: "Success to football, irrespective of class or creed."

Paul Brown, 2012

"I must confess that I have myself a strong predilection for football."

Football

J. D., 1887

~

SIGNS here and there are beginning to crop up
of the approaching winter. Boys are already
gathering thorns from the cut hedges against the
great fifth of November. The stacks in the hag-
gard have been thatched and made neat and
trim for the coming storms, so that not a crevice
may be left for the ingress of the searching snow
and the beating sleet. Good people everywhere
are beginning to lay aside their summer costumes and talk of the winter fashions. Orchards
have been relieved of their heavy burdens and
look desolate and forsaken. Thrifty house-
keepers have been getting in trucks of coals, and
grates that have lain idle for many months are
once more all ablaze. In old country towns the
street lamps have again come into requisition,
and are lighted by seven in the evening, when
there has been no moon to take the business out
of their hand. Daring the late heavy rains persons ill advised and impatient, devoid of experience and sound judgment through lack of years,

although mighty fine fellows in their own estimation, went gadding about open-mouthed, and
saying that we should have no more warm
weather, and might as well make up our minds
at once to face the winter. My old friend and I
have been comparing notes, and have come to
the conclusion, that, like as not, we shall have a
St. Michael's summer; or failing that, why, then,
a St. Martin's,[1] which will put us well on towards
Christmas and the merry times of the closing
year. He is, however, always very chary about
the weather, as becomes an old man who can call
to mind times without number when prophecies
or forecasts, both of his own and others, have
proved miserable failures, and enough to blast a
man's reputation for foresight, were it not that
both people in general and the weather itself
take little notice thereof, as trivialities beneath
consideration. Every morning almost I consult
him as to the likelihood of a fine day, but he will
seldom suffer himself to be driven beyond a
"humble opinion", and that even with some
qualifications and reservations, such as may let
him down easily at our next encounter should
the skies have proved unfavourable.

Whenever I see the goals set up in a
neighbouring field for football, I feel at once that

---

[1] Extended "Indian" summers lasting until St. Michael's
Day (29 September) or St. Martin's Day (11 November).

I must get into my winter ventures, and whether it be through imagination or a steady fall in the thermometer, I am sure to catch a chill if I do not forthwith obey the warning. My friend was saying the other evening, when we were surveying, after he had knocked off work and had had his tea, a stirring game among some thirty or forty young fellows and boys, that he can mind of football ever since he was little. But, then, said he, it was only played once or twice a year among men folk.

There was always a great set-to on Shrove Tuesday—he called it Pancake Tuesday—between different parishes. It was a sturdy fight, and many shins were broken; but it served folk to talk about for many a week afterwards.

Now, however, they must be playing whenever a lot of idle fellows can be got together. What was to come of the world if it went on as it was going he could not tell. It was his "candid opinion"—my friend was somewhat ruffled in his temper; for, as I afterwards found, he had had an obstinate tiff with his wife about the day of the month—that nobody in these days was saving a halfpenny of money, and if half the country were sold up at this very moment they could not pay twenty shillings to the pound.

When he was young, men and women lived sparsely, and were careful as to what they gave either to their backs or to their bellies, and could lay by something for old age or a rainy day. If it was not wanted by themselves they were pleased to have something to leave to those who came after them, even if was not more than a score or two of old spade-ace guineas to bury them decently and leave something over. They talked of "funeral reform", so the Vicar had told him, but it was his "private opinion" that if they went on as they had been going, riding in railways to see every tomfoolery that was stirring, and dressing like lords and ladies, their funerals would not need any reform, for there would be nothing to the fore wherewith to bury them at all. The question used to be, how much can we decently lay by. The sole thing now which gives anyone a second thought is simply, where can we go, or what can we buy, or how much can we get into debt. Words of Scripture were not minded now-a-days. We had become far too enlightened for such plain truths, and the world was going on in such a whirligig that a smash must come as sure as his name was Tommy Simpson. Here, after having inquired for the day of the month, and finding that he was right, the good man walked off in a mighty toss, vowing that his old wife should never hear the last of it.

But despite my friend's candid opinions about "the world being out of joint", and his own bad terms with it, I must confess that I have myself a strong predilection for football, and that, too, none the less because I can be only an onlooker, and no more as of old mingle in the stirring and fluctuating struggles of the game. In the first place, it brings into play all the wits of a man's mind and every sinew of his body, so that it is at once wholesome and invigorating to both. It is, in short, a mimic battle, and a good captain will not only look to the idiosyncrasies of his men and their staying power, but will be sure also to pay due regard to their proper disposition in the field, with an eye to the weak and strong points in the array of his adversaries. When once the ball is off every man becomes strained with attention, conflict, and excitement, nor does this cease for a single moment until the goal has been passed and victory proclaimed. How great has been the commotion and intense strain of the combatants may be gathered from the aspect of the field the moment the game is up. There is no longer now the eager uproar and shouting and struggle; the hot roll of the tide of battle now here, now there in such swift succession; the dreadful and agonising nearness of victory first at one goal then at the other; the horrible rush of some Ajax, son of Tydeus,[2] into the very centre of

---

[2] Ajax was the son of Telamon. The son of Tydeus was Diomedes (Greek mythology).

the whirlpool, and the crash and fall in one struggling mass of legs and arms and heads, while some adroit fellow, swift of foot like Achilles, the son of Peleus, whips off the ball, again to be intercepted by some outlying wing of light-armed waylayers. This is all over and at once.

The combatants fall away to whatever seat or support they can find, panting, gasping, and running with perspiration, presenting the very likeness of men who had been in actual warfare, but who, nevertheless, only needed a brief rest before beginning again the manful struggle for victory. Even the onlookers, who had followed the contest with an eager and sympathetic eye, feel almost as if they themselves had been in the real conflict, and now require something whereon to rest and ease the real tension of their minds and the imaginary exhaustion of their bodies.

It is true there are bodily dangers in football, and some serious accidents from time to time occur, which make timid persons cry out against the whole business. Perhaps it will not be believed, but there are more severe and more frequent accidents at cricket than at football. I myself have suffered three in the former for one in the latter.

However this may be, there can be no one who will not admit that the spice of danger in football adds greatly to the intrinsic worth of the game as an exercise well suited to call forth all the energies both of body and mind. It is an excellent discipline in coolness, courage, and temper, for these are indispensible to any one who would excel in the pastime. It is to be regretted that no such game as we know it was known to the ancient Greeks and Romans, for then we should have had the merits thereof sung in a manner worthy of the subject, among the funeral games of Hector or Anchises, by Homer and Virgil.[3]

Newcastle Weekly Courant, 21 October 1887

---

[3] Homer included the funeral games of Patroclus, slain by Hector, in the Iliad, and Virgil included the funeral games of Anchises in his Aeneid (Greek mythology).

Playing Up

C. W. Alcock, 1869

~

FOOTBALL is a game which, from the very
nature of its constitution, necessitates the undi-
vided attention of every player engaged, be he
great or small, fast or slow, whether his post be
one of the greatest importance, or whether the
position assigned to him be one of general utility.
Unlike cricket, where with an adverse fate it
may happen that for hours one may be suffering
from the ennui consequent on the protracted stay
made by two batsmen, or the occupancy of some
position in the field whereunto the ball never
comes, football affords scope and latitude for,
nay, requires the most unremitting zeal of every
participator in the sport, from the very commencement until the finish of the game. Every
player would do well to remember that the
smallest *faux pas* on the part of any single individual might influence and decide the whole
fortunes of a match, and any remissness or want
of energy during the course of the play might
enable the opposite side to convert into a drawn

game what might perhaps, with more assiduity on the part of the assailants, have proved a reverse.

First, then, let me impress on all the absolute necessity of "playing up" throughout the game, a piece of advice which appeals as forcibly to the most practised exponents of football art, as to the veriest tyro in the usages of the sport. "What thy hand findeth to do, do it with thy might," is an axiom which may, without undergoing the charge of profanity, prove useful advice on this point. Where victory depends so much on the unison with which each member of a body works, as is the case of a football team, it behoves all to strain every nerve to contribute to the joint success. Each player represents a component part of a huge machine, which cannot work to any purpose without the co-operation of every minute particle associated in its composition, and which is thrown into disorder on the first case of negligence, or the most trifling flaw in any portion of the works.

To play for his side, and not for individual fame and glory, as is far too often the case, even with the most popular performers, ought to be the North Star of any young performer's aspirations. How often has the thorough co-operation of the various members of a side, boasting of no especial players of repute, overcome the disorganised attacks of an enemy richer in individual skill. A game is never lost until it is won, and at any time the fickle goddess Fortune may smile upon the efforts of the deserving.

"Play up" until the last moment, and never relax the energy of your attack, always sacrificing your own personal gratification to the general weal, is in my opinion the first and golden rule of football—a rule which is too often lost sight of in the eager thirst after the applause of the "gallery", always showered down on "flashy" play. Any one who has watched football games with any degree of care will have noticed how few players seem to consider and study the welfare of the side to which they belong; how rarely it is that a player, whom in possession of the ball, ever thinks of passing it to one of his own party, even when harassed by several enemies; how exceptional are the instances of a player "dribbling" the ball along the side of the ground, kicking it into the centre, and thus transferring his hopes of success to some fellow struggler, who has perhaps been cautiously watching every movement of the ball in order to take advantage of some weak point in the enemy's armour.

Second only perhaps in importance to the mainspring of football, as I consider "playing up", is the grand and essential principle of "backing

up". By "backing up" of course I shall be understood to mean the following closely on a fellow
player to assist him, if required, or to take on the
ball in case of his being attacked, or otherwise
prevented from continuing his onward course.

The Football Annual, 1869

C. W. "Charlie" Alcock (1842-1907) is regarded by many as
the founding father of modern football. A skilled player, he
was elected to the committee of the Football Association in
1866, and appointed secretary in 1870. Alcock instigated the
FA Cup competition in the following year, and won the first
tournament as captain of Wanderers. He also instigated and
umpired the first official international football match,
between Scotland and England, in 1872. He subsequently
played five times for England. Alcock, born in Sunderland,
compiled his Football Annuals from 1868.

Cup Ties and Professionalism

An Interview with Tinsley Lindley, 1888

~

TO-DAY is a great one for footballers. The final tie for the Challenge Cup, given by the Football Association, is to be decided at the Oval between the Preston North End Club and the West Bromwich Albion. Both teams have been in careful training for some time, and, although the North Enders are the popular favourites, it is expected that the Midlanders will run them closely. Nearly all the players are professionals, and as such, of course, receive payment for their services. A certain section of amateurs has resented the introduction of such an element into the game, and it is now just *on the tapis*[4] among a number of them to start a cup of their own and boycott professionals. The controversy has engendered a great deal of bitterness, and possibly forebodes a large secession from the present method of competition from the cup. Hearing of the probable split, our correspondent interviewed

---

[4] On the carpet (French), or under consideration.

Mr. T. Lindley, the captain of the Cambridge
Football Eleven, on the thorny points of the
subject. Mr. Lindley is considered by many to be
the finest "forward" of the day. At school he was
a prominent player, and has been in the Varsity
Eleven during the whole of his residence.

"What sort of match do you think it will be at
the Oval, Mr. Lindley?" inquired our correspondent.

"Very close, I think. Preston North End, to my
mind, have a better combination and also the
better defence, while the West Bromwich Albion
are very neat in regard to passing the ball. [Jem]
Bayliss, too, will keep his forwards well together.
A point to their credit is that they are all local
men."

"How do you account for such small crowds in
London in proportion to those North of the
Trent?"

"I think there will be an exceptionally big
crowd this time, probably 12,000, as the Boat
Race ought to increase the number. It is only for
exceptional matches that so many gather in the
North, and secondary matches have very little
interest taken in them. Again, 'gates' in London
are a shilling, while in the North they are six-
pence and threepence."

"What has contributed most to the rapid rise
of the Association game?"

MR. T. LINDLEY

"Well, I think many people joined the Association because they thought Rugby dangerous. Association, too, is much more pretty to look at, and the rules are simpler, so that an outsider can enter into them thoroughly. Preston North End were once a Rugby team."

"Don't you think the cup has materially assisted?"

"Yes, it has. The excitement caused by such contests has undoubtedly tended to increase the popularity of the game, both among spectators and players. It has also been the means of raising what would have been second-rate clubs into notice, and bringing them into first-class company, and consequently better fixtures. The cup, of course, has had a great deal to do with bringing professionalism to the front."

"Has professionalism been a source of trouble or injury to the game?"

"Well, I don't think it has done much injury in first-class matches, but in second-rate teams it has. Many of these are too mercenary. Still, if properly managed, I don't think professionalism a trouble. You see, at cricket they don't define the distinctions so badly as at football, and the amateur and professional have each their place. Personally, though, I don't lay so much on distinctions."

"What, then, are the most objectionable points

in professionals?"

"Well, their style of play. They know they have to win, and are more reckless, whereas the amateur plays for pleasure. With professionals, the club must get money, and if they don't win, their 'gate' falls off and they fall into debt."

"Are they paid as well as cricketers?"

"Oh no! You see, a cricketer receives his £5 a match, while the footballer gets about 30s. per week; but has a situation generally found for him as well."

"What are the good points?"

"Well, they have a good combination, are very 'tricky', and can 'dribble' well. Still, I think a picked team of amateurs equal to them."

"Do you think amateurs will go in for a cup of their own?"

"Well, there is an agitation in favour of such, but it would not be carried out if the Football Association opposed. I think that, if an amateur team enter for an amateur cup, they should not be disqualified for entering for the National Cup."

"You do not favour class distinctions, then?"

"No! Certainly not. I have no opposition to social position whatsoever, but only to some of the outcomes of professionalism."

"Will it be a southern cup or an amateur one?"

"I think it will be an amateur and not confined

to the southern counties."

"Just a point or two on the game, Mr. Lindley, if you please. What would you recommend to a team for success?"

"Well, combination in every position, and no individual play. If you have combination thoroughly carried out among 'backs' as well as 'forwards' you must succeed."

"What would you say are the chief duties of a 'centre-forward'?"

"A great thing, of course, is to keep all the forwards together and to use more 'passing' than 'dribbling', especially watching well, so as to pass to the outside 'wings'. When the forwards are not level with him then he should go on by himself, and, when within about fifteen or twenty yards, he should go on by himself, and when within about fifteen or twenty yards he should 'shoot' at goal at every opportunity. A 'centre-forward' should be as far forward as possible when attacking, but always 'on-side'. On defending, he should fall back and assist the 'halves'."

"How about the 'wings', then?"

"I think outside 'wings' should not wait till they get too close to the goal line before 'centring', but rather that they pass to the inside man, who would then have a better opportunity to 'shoot' or pass to the 'centre-forward'."

Here the interview ended, owing to the

engagements of the Light Blue captain, else-where, pressing him for time.

Pall Mall Gazette, 24 March 1888

Tinsley Lindley (1865-1940) was a highly-regarded England captain and centre-forward. He scored 14 goals in 13 matches for his country between 1886 and 1891. At the time of this interview he played for Cambridge University (the "Light Blues"), but he was shortly to sign for Nottingham Forest.

The Fight for the Association Cup

West Bromwich Albion v Preston North End, 1888

~

THE West-End streets of London wore quite a holiday look on Saturday morning. There was the crowd of sprucely-dressed gentlemen from the universities, attired in the tallest of collars, the glossiest of hats, and the shiniest of patent leathers, who were up for the boat race. There was the crowd of gentlemen, not quite so spruce, from the provinces, who were visiting the metropolis to shout for their men at the Oval.

In the great world of athletics the final fight for the silver trophy of the football association is yearly increasing in interest. However hard a struggle the two crews make, it can only be seen in bits by the multitude. The football match is contested in a small area, and can be watched from beginning to end. So while the boat race is a pretext for a picnic, the football match offers a most inspiriting form of excitement. On Saturday afternoon Kennington Oval presented a remarkable sight long before the two teams were due on

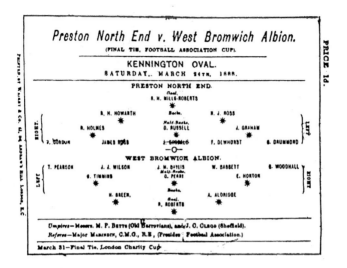

the field of battle. As early as one o'clock there was a steady stream of cabs running towards the famous cricket ground, and at three o'clock there was not a seat to be had. Some estimated the crowd at 20,000. Whatever the exact numbers the spectacle of those solid banks of human beings, rising row above row, on the four sides of the square was a remarkable tribute to the extraordinary interest in the result.

After months of hard fighting the final battle for the football championship was left to be fought by eleven doughty Prestonians and eleven equally doughty footballers from Birmingham. The 20,000 people on the ground were a mere drop in the ocean compare with the countless thousands who were waiting for the result in

Preston and Birmingham and in dozens of murky towns in Lancashire, Yorkshire, the Midlands, to say nothing of Scotland. To judge by the movements of the telegraph boys, who were running in and out over five minutes during the progress of the game, the millions out of London must have been able to follow every point of the game as closely as we did ourselves who were sitting at the press table.

It was really most melancholy to reflect that, in the face of so much earnestness and such savage enthusiasm, both sides could not win, for when after a gallant fight the Prestonians were beaten, the looks on the faces of their supporters were suicidal. If they drowned their sorrows in the flowing bowl, let us forgive them. Preston at six o'clock on Saturday evening must have been a town of mourning. The love of battle is great in the manufacturing towns in the North. Long days of arduous labour in the mill or the foundry leave little time for pleasure, and the manufacturing town presents few amusements for its inhabitants. So it is not difficult to understand the enormous popularity of football in the North and the Midlands.

When the clock struck three on Saturday afternoon the Oval was packed by an excited but extremely good-tempered multitude. The fog had disappeared before the benign influence of a bright sun, there was no wind, and it was actually warm. There was half an hour to wait so, after the manner of a big meeting, the crowd burst into song, and the strains of Two Lovely Black Eyes,[5] Rule Britannia, and other ditties filled the air. At last the eleven Prestonians appeared in blue knickerbockers and white guernseys, quickly followed by all the Bromwich Albions in white ducks and blue and white guernseys, all, except the goal keepers, with bare legs protected by whalebone pads in case of a chance hack. The silver cup for which they were about to contend was placed on a table in a conspicuous portion of the field, as if any such incentive was needed when the eyes of Great Britain were upon them. Major Mandarin was the referee, Mr. Betts and Mr. Clegg the umpires, each armed with a little flag and a whistle.

In a minute the men were at work for the next hour and a half, with a brief respite of five minutes a most exciting struggle took place among a hurricane of criticism, much of it difficult for the layman to follow. Bill, Jack, Bob, Nick and Dick were constantly appealed to by their friends with a familiarity which was anything but contemptuous to do this or the other. And the champions were mightily encouraged by the support of their

---

[5] Popular comic song by music hall singer Charles Coburn.

friends and admirers, who had come up in special trains to give them a hand. Every change, every fine bit of dribbling, every pass, every run, every shot at goal, was the signal for a deafening roar. The men seemed to be as ready with their heads as their feet, and never scrupled to receive the leather projectile on their cranium if they saw an advantage to be gained. At last the "Brummies" got a goal. This only made the bold Prestonians play up the more fiercely, and presently their endeavours were rewarded by a goal. Then came the tug of war. But the luck was with the "Brums", who got another, and then their opponents seemed to lose heart, and never had another chance. It was a splendid battle, worth travelling a long way to see.

Pall Mall Gazette, 26 March 1888

The 1888 FA Cup Final was played on 24 March in controversial circumstances. Referee Major Francis Mandarin was accused of favouring all-English underdogs West Brom over Preston's team of 'Invincibles', which included several Scottish professionals. George Woodhall scored first for West Brom, Fred Dewhurst equalised for Preston, and West Brom captain Jem Bayliss scored the winner.

A History of Football

Montague Shearman, 1887

~

THE game of football is undoubtedly the oldest of all the English national sports. For at least six centuries the people have loved the rush and struggle of the rude and manly game, and kings with their edicts, divines with their sermons, scholars with their cultured scorn, and wits with their ridicule have failed to keep the people away from the pastime they enjoyed. Cricket may at times have excited greater interest amongst the leisured classes; boat-races may have drawn larger crowds of spectators from distant places; but football, which flourished for centuries before the arts of boating or cricketing were known, may fairly claim to be not only the oldest and the most characteristic, but the most essentially popular sport of England.

Football has now developed into a variety of highly organised games, and the difficulty of finding its actual origin is as great as that of discovering the commencement of athletic contests. If men have run races ever since the creation, it may almost be said that they have played at ball since the same date.

It is scarcely necessary to say that the Greeks and Romans both played at ball; even as early as the days of the Odyssey we find Nausicaa and her maidens "playing at ball". What is perhaps of more importance is that the Greeks had a game in which the kind of ball known as the *arpaston* was employed, and this game bore a rough resemblance to football in England.[6] The players of one side had to carry the ball over a line defended by the other, by any means in their power. The arpaston was a small ball. The Romans, however, had another pastime with a large inflated ball, the *follis*. The follis, however, was undoubtedly a handball, and the game was probably the same as the *baloon ball* of the middle ages, which consisted in simply striking into the air and "keeping up" a large windy ball, a sport which is still to be seen exhibited with great skill in Paris. All this, however, has little concern with football, except that it is pretty clear that the follis or baloon ball was the same that is used in the game of football, and it is a matter of some importance to discover whether football is merely a game brought by Roman civilisation into Britain, or a native product. It is

---

[6] This game is referred to in other sources as *episkyros*.

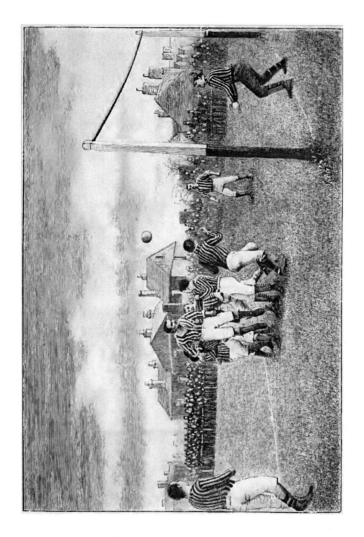

THE ASSOCIATION GAME
From a photograph by G. Mitchell

hardly to be believed that it should never have occurred to a man playing with the follis to kick it with his foot when his arms were tired, but be that as it may, we know of no mention of a game played by the Romans where the feet were used to kick the ball, and of the game known from the middle ages to the present time as football no trace can be found in any country but our own.

Before we come to a definite record relating to football, it may perhaps be worth while to point out that the legends connected with football at some of its chief centres point to its immense antiquity. At Chester, where hundreds of years ago the people played on the Roodee[7] on Shrove Tuesday, the contemporary chroniclers state that the first ball used was the head of a Dane who had been captured and slain and whose head was kicked about for sport. At Derby, where (also on Shrove Tuesday) the celebrated match of which we shall have to speak later on was played for centuries, there was a legend (as stated in [Stephen] Glover's History of Derby) that the game was a memorial of a victory over the Romans in the third century. These and other signs, apart from any written record, would be sufficient to show the antiquity of the sport.

FitzStephen [a Canterbury monk], who wrote

---

[7] Chester racecourse.

in the 12th century, makes an allusion to a game which there is very little doubt must be football. He says that the boys "annually upon Shrove Tuesday go into the fields and play at the well-known game of ball". The words are of course vague, but they undoubtedly refer to one special game and not to general playing with balls, and no other game of ball is ever known to have been specially connected with Shrove Tuesday, which there is abundant material to show was afterwards the great "football day" in England for centuries. There is also ample proof of the fondness of the London boys and 'prentices for football in succeeding centuries, which makes the inference irresistible that the writer refers to football. It is also noticeable that FitzStephen probably refrains from describing the game because it was too well known throughout the country to require a description.

By the reign of Edward II, we find not only that football was popular in London, but that so many people joined in the game when it was being played in the streets that peaceable merchants had to request the king to put down its practice. Accordingly, in 1314, Edward II, on April 13, issued a proclamation forbidding the game as leading to a breach of the peace: "Forasmuch as there is great noise in the city caused by hustling over large balls... from which many evils might arise which God forbid: we command and forbid on behalf of the king, on pain of imprisonment, such game to be used in the city in future."

As football acquired royal animadversion as early as 1314, it would seem that the early footballers played no less vigorously, if with less courtesy, than the players of the present day.

There can be no doubt that from the earliest days football was an obstreperous and disreputable member of the family of British Sports, and indeed almost an "habitual criminal" in its character, a fact to which we owe most of the earliest references to the game, as many of these records refer to little else but crimes and grievances. In 1349 football is mentioned by its present name in a statute of Edward III, who objected to the game not so much for itself, but as tending to discourage the practice of shooting, upon which the military strength of England largely depended. The King writing in that year to the Sheriffs of London, says that "the skill at shooting with arrows was almost totally laid aside for the purpose of various useless and unlawful games", and the Sheriffs are thereupon commanded to suppress "such idle practices". The injunction can hardly have been of much avail, however, for forty years afterwards Richard II passed a similar statute (c. 1389) forbidding throughout the kingdom "all playing at tennise, football, and other games called corts, dice, casting of the stone, kailes, and other such importune games". The same statute had to be re-enacted by Henry IV in 1401, so that it is tolerably obvious that, like some other statutes still in force and relating to sporting matters, it was more honoured in the breach than in the observance. Football was evidently too strong for the House of Lancaster, and all attempts to coerce the merry Englishman into giving it up were hopeless failures. Similar measures in Scotland in the next century altogether failed to persuade the Scottish sportsmen to give up football and golf. In 1457 James III decreed that four times every year reviews and displays of weapons were to be held, and "footballe and golfe be utterly cryed down and not to be used"; but as in 1491 his successor had again to prohibit golf and football by a fresh statute providing that "in na place of this realme ther be used futeball, golfe, or other sik unprofitable sportes", it appears that in Scotland as well as in England football was strong enough to defy the law. In the sixteenth century the House of Tudor again tried to do what the House of Lancaster had failed in doing, and Henry VIII not only re-enacted the old statute against cards, dice, and other "importune games", but rendered it a penal offence by statute for anybody to keep a house or ground devoted to these sporting purposes.

The English people, however, both in town and country would have their football, and throughout the sixteenth century football was as popular a pastime amongst the lower orders as it has ever been before or since. The game was fiercely attacked, as some of the succeeding extracts will show, and the same extracts will suggest that the nature of the game played at that period rendered the attacks not altogether unreasonable. In 1508, [Alexander] Barclay in his fifth eclogue affords evidence that football was as popular in the country as in the town. Says Barclay:

The sturdie plowman, lustie, strong, and bold,
Overcometh the winter with driving the foote-
ball,
Forgetting labour and many a grievous fall.

Not long after this, Sir Thomas Elyot in his *Boke Called the Governour*, inveighs against football, as being unfit for gentlemen owing to the violence with which it was played. Sir Thomas, however, had a courtly hatred of anything energetic: he prefers archery to tennis, and the following remarks therefore about skittles, quoits and football, are only such as one would expect. "Verilie," he says, "as for two the laste (pinnes and koyting) be to be utterly abjected of all noble men in like wise foote-balle wherein is nothing but beastlie furie and exstreme violence whereof procedeth hurte, and consequently rancour and malice do remain with them that be wounded, wherfore it is to be put in perpetual silence." Doubtless "hurte procedeth" from football upon occasions, but if there had been "nothing in" football but beastly fury, it would hardly have held its own so bravely to the present time. Sir Thomas Elyot had some foundation for his strictures, as the coroner's records of the day show; but before we proceed to give these, we should describe in some sort the nature of the game as it was played in the sixteenth century. There is no trace in ancient times of anything like the modern "Association game", where the players only kick the ball and may not strike it with their hands, throw it or run with it. Probably the name "football" was first used to describe the ball itself, and meant a ball which was big enough to be kicked and could be kicked with the foot. The game of football was the game played with this kind of ball, and it was simple to an extreme degree. The goals were two bushes, posts, houses, or any objects fixed upon at any distance apart from a few score yards to a few miles. The ball was placed mid-way between the two goals at starting, the players (of any number) divided into two sides, and it was the business of either side to get the ball by force or strategy up to or through the goal of the opposite side. When confined to a street, or field of play, it is obvious that the sport was the original form of what is now known as the Rugby Union game. At the times before any settled rules of play were known, and before football had been civilised, the game must of necessity have been a very rough one, and an unfriendly critic may well have thought that the ball had very little to do with the game, just as the proverbial Frenchman is unable to see what the fox has to do with fox-hunting. Undoubtedly the game of football was until quite recent times a vulgar and unfashion-able sport, as indeed were cricket, boat-racing, and most other athletic pastimes. For many centuries in England any pedestrian sport which was not immediately connected with knightly skill was considered unworthy of a gentleman of equestrian rank, and this will account in a great measure for the adverse criticisms of football which proceed from writers of aristocratic posi-tion.

That Elizabethan football was dangerous to life, limb, and property, is made plain by many records. The Middlesex County Records contain several entries which are of interest to the histo-rian of football, and show how rough was the game. In the eighteenth year of the reign of good Queen Bess, the grand jury of the county found a true bill:

Malefactors to the number of one hundred assembled themselves unlawfully and playd a certain unlawful game called foote-ball, by means of which unlawful game there was amongst them a great affray likely to result in homicides and serious accidents.

In the 23rd year of Elizabeth, football seems to have led to something more serious than a breach of the peace:

Coroner's inquisition — post-mortem taken in view of the body of Roger Ludforde, yoman there lying dead with verdict of jurors that Nicholas Martyn and Richard Turvey, both yomen, were playing with other persons at foote-ball in the field called Evanses field at Southmyms, when the said Roger Ludford cried out, "Cast hym over the hedge", indicating that he meant Nicholas Martyn, who replied, "Come thou and do yt." That thereupon Roger Ludforde ran towards the ball with the intention to kick it, whereupon Nicholas Martyn with the fore-part of his right arm and Richard Turvey with the fore-part of his left arm struck Roger Ludforde on the fore-part of the body under the breast, giving him a mortal blow and concussion of which he died within a quarter of an hour, and that Nicholas and Richard in this manner feloniously slew the said Roger.

Some years later, the Manchester Lete Roll contains a resolution, dated October 12, 1608:

That whereas there hath been heretofore great disorder in our towne of Manchester, and the inhabitants thereof greatly wronged and charged with makinge and amendinge of their glasse windows broken yearelye and spoyled by a companye of lewd and disordered psons vsing that unlawfull exercise of playinge with the ffote-ball in ye streets of ye sd toune breakinge many men's windowes and glasse at their plesures and other great enormyties. Therefore, wee of this jurye doe order that no manner of psons hereafter shall play or use the footeball in any street within the said toune of Manchester.

These extracts not only show that the number of players was unlimited, but that the game was played in the street and over hedges in the country, although it was still unlawful by statute. It is hardly to be wondered at that the citizens of great towns objected to promiscuous scrimmaging in the streets in front of their windows. The records of the Corporation of the City of London contain two entries in the time of Elizabeth, (November 27, 1572, and November 7, 1581), of a proclamation having been made that "no foteballe play be used or suffered within the City of London and the liberties thereof upon pain of imprisonment". In spite of this, however, we still hear in later times of football in the streets.

It was only to be expected that the grave and demure Puritans, who objected to all sports not only for themselves, but because they were played on Sundays, should have a particular and violent objection to football, for football even when played on a week-day does not seem to be wholly compatible with a meek and chastened spirit. The strictures passed by [Phillip] Stubbes, the earnest author of the Anatomic of Abuses in the Realme of England, show pretty clearly the Puritan attitude towards football. Amongst other reasons for concluding that the end of the world was at hand in 1583, he gives the convincing reason that "football playing and other develishe pastimes" were practised on the Sabbath day.

One other hostile criticism of football in that age should be mentioned. King James I, in his *Basilikon Doron*, or Manual of Precepts for his Son and Successor, praises some other sports as good for the body, but makes a reservation of football. "From this count", he says, "I debar all rough and violent exercise as the football meeter for laming than for making able the users thereof."

Football, however, survived criticism as it had before survived repressive legislation. Throughout the whole of the sixteenth century, and that part of the seventeenth century before Puritanism gained the upper hand, it remained one of the favourite sports of the people. About 1600, football was still in full vigour. Amongst the country sports mentioned by [wandering minstrel] Randel Holme, the Lancashire men challenge anybody to:

Try it out at football by the shinnes.

Some of their talented successors in the county who have figured at the Oval upon the occasion of the Football Jubilee Festival and elsewhere, are still capable, it appears, of upholding the boast of their bard; but times are changed, and as their association players wear "shinguards", the game is no longer tried out by the shins alone. Other and better bards than Randel Holme have spoken of football. Shakespeare, in his Comedy of Errors, has:

Am I so round with you as you with me
That like a football you do spurn me thus?
You spurn me hence and he will spurn me hither;
If I last in this service you must case me in
leather.

Another extract too from King Lear shows that "tripping" and "hacking over" were then regular parts of the game.

Lear. Do you bandy looks with me, you rascal?

"Bandy" was originally another name for hockey, and to "bandy" a ball meant to strike it backwards and forwards, which may account for the context.

Steward. I'll not be strucken, my lord.
Kent. Nor tripped neither, you base football
player (tripping up on his heels).
Lear. I thank thee, fellow.

Lear's faithful courtier then is made by Shakespeare to understand the art of "tripping", which seems significant.

As far as can be gathered from extracts, taken in their chronological order, it appears certain that the triumph of Puritanism considerably reduced the popularity of football. The political ascendency of this ascetic creed was short, but the hold that it took upon the manners and feelings of the nation not only put a stop in a great measure to Sunday football, but rendered the game less acceptable upon other days. From the slight number of references made to football by eighteenth-century writers, it would appear evident that in that century the game was no longer of national popularity. In London, however, in the reign of Charles II, football still appears to have gone on merrily, and this was only to be expected, for Charles was a great patron of athletic sport; indeed, there is a precedent for the royal patronage of football which was seen when the Prince of Wales visited Kennington Oval, in March, 1886. One hundred and ninety-five years before this date Charles II attended a match which was played between his own servants and those of the Duke of Albemarle. Some years before this too (1665) [Samuel] Pepys tells us that on January 2, there being a great frost, the streets were full of footballs. Modern footballers give up their games in frosty weather for fear of accidents upon the hard ground, but the 'prentice lads who played in the streets were probably doing little more than "punt-about" to keep themselves warm. Even the 'prentices of the period, however, were occupying their leisure hours with more serious pursuits than football.

The great historian of English sports, Joseph Strutt, gives but a short description of the game of football, but from what he says it is evident that at the time he wrote (1801) the game was fast decaying. "Football," he says, "is so called because the ball is driven about with the feet instead of the hands." The following is the only description he gives of the game:

When a match at football is made an equal number of competitors take the field and stand between two goals placed at a distance of eighty or an hundred yards the one from the other. The goal is usually made with two sticks driven into the ground about two or three feet apart. The ball, which is commonly made of a blown bladder and cased with leather, is delivered in the midst of the ground, and the object of each party is to drive it through the goal of their antagonists, which being achieved the game is won. The abilities of the performers are best displayed in attacking and defending the goals; and hence the pastime was more frequently called a goal at football than a game at football. When the exercise becomes exceeding violent the players kick each other's shins without the least ceremony, and some of them are overthrown at the hazard of their limbs.

What is perhaps the most significant part of Strutt's description is that he says, "The game was formerly much in vogue among the common people, though of late years it seems to have fallen into disrepute and is but little practised." Indeed, the decline in the popularity of the game which Strutt noticed at the opening of this century seems to have gone steadily on for the next fifty years, in England at any rate.

In Scotland, however, it appears to have been more flourishing. [Sir Walter] Scott could hardly have written in the Lay of the Last Minstrel:—

Some drive the jolly bowl about.
With dice and draughts some chase the day,
And some with many a merry shout.
In riot, revelry, and rout,
Pursue the football play

—if he had not seen plenty of football in his time. Indeed, [William] Hone assists us in an account of a great football match in Scotland with which Scott was personally concerned: "On Tuesday, the 5th of December, 1815, a great football match took place at Carterhaugh, Ettrick Forest (a spot classical in minstrelsy) betwixt the Ettrick men and the men of Yarrow, the one party backed by the Earl of Home and the other by Sir Walter Scott, sheriff of the forest, who wrote two songs for the occasion." One of the songs is given in extenso, but space forbids our quoting more than a couple of verses:

From the brown crest of Newark its summons extending,
Our signal is waving in smoke and in flame;
And each forester blithe from his mountain descending
Bounds light o'er the heather to join in the game.

Then strip lads and to it, though sharp be the weather,
And if, by mischance, you should happen to fall,
There are worse things in life than a tumble on heather,
And life is itself but a game at football.

Luckily, however, though football steadily decreased in popularity throughout the first half of this century, it was rather in a state of dormancy than of collapse, and was not long in picking up again when in the fifties the revival came from the public schools. It is not too much to say that the present football movement can be directly traced to the public schools and to them alone, though, in a great many centres, when the revival came the game was still known not only as a game for boys, but as a pastime for men. In many corners of England, indeed, the old time-honoured game, without rules or limit to the number of players or size of ground, was being carried on, and even is carried on to the present day. The most celebrated, however, of these time-honoured games was that at Derby. The following is the account of the Derby game given by Glover in his History of Derbyshire published in 1829:

The contest lies between the parishes of St. Peter's and All Saints, and the goals to which the ball is taken are Nun's Mill for the latter and the Gallows balk on the Normanton Road for the former. None of the other parishes in the borough take any direct part in the contest, but the inhabitants of all join in the sport, together with persons from all parts of the adjacent country. The players are young men from eighteen to thirty or upwards, married as well as single, and many veterans who retain a relish for the sport are occasionally seen in the very heat of the conflict. The game commences in the market-place, where the partisans of each parish are drawn up on each side, and about noon a large ball is tossed up in the midst of them. This is seized upon by some of the strongest and most active men of each party. The rest of the players immediately close in upon them and a solid mass is formed. It then becomes the object of each party to impel the course of the crowd towards their particular goal. The struggle to obtain the ball, which is carried in the arms of those who have possessed themselves of it, is then violent, and the motion of the human tide heaving to and fro without the least regard to consequences is tremendous. Broken shins, broken heads, torn coats, and lost hats are amongst the minor accidents of this fearful contest, and it frequently happens that persons fall owing to the intensity of the pressure, fainting and bleeding beneath the feet of the surrounding mob. But it would be difficult to give an adequate idea of this ruthless sport. A Frenchman passing through Derby remarked, that if Englishmen called this playing, it would be impossible to say what they would call fighting. Still the crowd is encouraged by respectable persons attached to each party, who take a surprising interest in the result of the day's sport, urging on the players with shouts, and even handing to those who are exhausted oranges and other refreshment. The object of the St. Peter's party is to get the ball into the water down the Morledge brook into the Derwent as soon as they can, while the All Saints party endeavour to prevent this and to urge the ball westward. The St. Peter players are considered to be equal to the best water spaniels, and it is certainly curious to see two or three hundred men up to their chins in the Derwent continually ducking each other. The numbers engaged on both sides exceed a thousand, and the streets are crowded with lookers-on. The shops are closed, and the town presents the aspect of a place suddenly taken by storm.

So far we have traced the history of football as it was played by the people at large, and have shown that it had a continued existence for at least six centuries as a recognised manly sport. We have seen also that at the end of the last and beginning of the present century, the game was certainly waning in popularity, and that the writers of the early part of this century are inclined to treat it as a sort of interesting relic of antiquity. To-day, however, football can be fairly described as once again the most thoroughly popular of all British sports. The game attracts as many spectators, and as many players in the winter, as the national sport of cricket in the summer. All that remains to complete the history of football is to describe the causes and progress of the modern revival of the game.

The present writer has already, in conjunction with Mr. J. E. Vincent, written a small book upon the history of football,[8] which has not only

---

[8] *Football: Its History for Five Centuries* (1885).

covered a good deal of the ground which has been traced in this chapter, but discusses the origin of the various forms of school football. The conclusion arrived at in that work was that "in each particular school the rules of the, game were settled by the capacity of the playground; and that as these were infinitely various in character so were the games various." It might also have been added that the Association game, or at least the various forms of game where kicking alone was allowed, and collaring and therefore running with the ball forbidden, also arose entirely in the schools, where either from the want of a sufficient playground, or from other causes, the old rough game was impracticable. There can be no doubt that the game which we have described in the preceding pages was not only risky to limb (that perhaps was a slight consideration for English schoolboys) when played upon a good grass plot, but when played in a walled-in space such as the cloisters of Charterhouse, or on a very small and confined playground with a flagged pavement, would have been probably dangerous to life. In any case too the collaring game must have been highly destructive to clothing of every description; and it is therefore small wonder that at the majority of schools the running, collaring and hacking game should have been tabooed, probably by order of the school authorities or the parents.

Now at the present day every large school has a good large grass playground either in the grounds of the school itself or within convenient reach; but in the olden times little or no provision for "playing fields" appears to have been made by pious or other founders. One school alone seems to have owned almost from its foundation a wide open grass playground of ample dimensions, and that school was Rugby; hence it happens, as we should have expected, that at Rugby School alone do we find that the original game survived almost in its primitive shape. Nor is it difficult to see how the "dribbling game" arose at schools where the playground was limited. Given a number of boys with that common vehicle of amusement a football, and no space where they could play the traditional game, they would soon learn to dribble it about with their feet for amusement and soon attain to skill and pace in their pastime. It would require very little ingenuity when the original game was impracticable to borrow the goals and touch-lines from the field game, and simply allow kicking as the only method of propulsion. In proportion therefore as the school was limited in the size of its playground we should expect to trace less of the old "friendlie fyghte" and more of the dribbling game. Again, we find the very examples which we should expect to prove our theory in the London schools. The Charterhouse boys had originally no ground but their cloisters to play in; we believe the Westminster boys were for a long time similarly ill provided with a playground; and it is from Charterhouse and Westminster that the dribbling game as it is played at present under Association rules came almost in its present form. At Winchester the ancient custom appears to have been to play football upon small strips round the edge of the "Meads", the centre being reserved for cricket, and it is from this practice that the peculiar characteristics of the Winchester game arose. There was no danger in shoving upon the Winchester strips of grass, so the shoving of the old game remained in the Winchester rules; and dribbling consequently remained at a discount. At Harrow, where there was probably more room, a large amount of catching and free kicking was allowed, but running and collaring found no place in the game. It is thus that we obtain the clearest illustrations of the theory that the different schools adapted the old game to the necessities of their own playgrounds. At Eton formerly the only original playground was a small field near the College buildings. Consequently their "field game" was chiefly a kicking game, but long-kicking and scrimmages were not barred, as they were of necessity bound to be at Charterhouse and at Westminster. The other Eton game, the well-known "wall-game", probably drew its rules and character from the space against the wall upon which it was played.

The different schools, in adopting as a pastime the national game of football in which any and every method of getting the ball through the goal was allowed, included only such parts of the game as were suitable to their ground, or to put the case in another way, eliminated from the game every characteristic which was necessarily unsuitable to the circumstances under which alone the game could be played. As far as we can discover, however, no school but Rugby played the old style of game where every player was allowed to pick up the ball and run with it, and every adversary could stop him by collaring. What causes led the Rugby authorities to differ from the managers of other schools it is difficult to see, but it is tolerably plain that the "Rugby game" was originally played at Rugby school alone, while other schools adopted more or less modified forms of the kicking game. That other schools did play football is clear enough from the annals of Eton, Westminster and Charterhouse, and private schools played the game also without doubt.

At no other public school, however, as far as

we are aware, was the running and collaring game kept up. At many of the other chief schools there were games where more or less "scrimmaging" was allowed, but at all of these the only method of propulsion allowed was kicking. Some schools allowed "free-kicking" and catching, some allowed while others disallowed the stopping of the ball with the hands, some allowed "off-side" play, and some forbade it. But until the revival of football came all the other public schools but Rugby played the game in which running with the ball was not allowed. Now as it was discovered as soon as attempts were made to codify and assimilate rules some quarter of a century ago, the essential distinction between the two entirely distinct games which are now played under the names of "Rugby Union" and "Association" football, is that in the former running with the ball, and therefore tackling, is allowed; in the other it is entirely forbidden. As soon as any running with the ball under however stringent conditions was permitted, the running became the important feature of the game, and no compromise between running and non-running games was possible.

The Association or "kicking" game came before the world from Eton, Harrow, Westminster, Charterhouse, and other schools where something of the same style of game was played. All these schools had rules differing in many essential characteristics from one another, but all agreeing in forbidding any seizing of the ball and running with it.

It is of course difficult to trace in any detail the steps by which both games gradually spread from the chief schools to the smaller schools, and from both to the public at large. From enquiries we have instituted it appears that between 1850 and 1860, the same period in which "Athletic Sports" were taking root in schools and colleges, all the schools adopted football as part of the regular athletic curriculum, and as the chief school game for the winter months. Gradually the old public school boys started the game again after they had left school, at the Universities and around the large towns. At Cambridge old members of the schools which played the dribbling game appear to have been indulging in matches as early as 1855: and about the same time the game was begun again regularly in Sheffield.

Two clubs, the Sheffield and Hallam clubs, were founded simultaneously in 1857. We believe, however, that a club which played the dribbling game under the title of the "Forest Club", and existed near Epping Forest, claimed before its untimely decease the honour of being the first football club of modern times. In 1858 some old Rugbeians and old boys of the

Blackheath Proprietary School started the famous Blackheath Club to play the Rugby game, and in the following year their great rivals in the game, the Richmond Club, came into existence. Soon after 1860 there was a great football "boom" at Sheffield, and several fresh clubs sprang up, and indeed from that time for the next fifteen years the Sheffielders could put an eleven into the field able to meet any other eleven in the kingdom.

Meantime in London several dribbling clubs were being established, the Crystal Palace in 1861 and the Civil Service and Barnes in 1862. So far the dribbling clubs were decidedly in the majority, as besides Richmond and Blackheath and the Harlequins we believe there were no other regularly constituted clubs playing the Rugby rules before 1863. In 1863 the first move towards football organisation was made, and after much exposition in the columns of the press of the necessity for assimilation of rules, an attempt was made in the autumn of that year by the leading London clubs to settle a uniform code of rules for all players. The suggested compromise between the essentially different games which were being played was to allow running either when the ball was caught on a fair catch, or caught on a bound, and it was even proposed before the committee which met to frame the

"compromise" rules that hacking and tripping
should be allowed when the adversary was running with the ball. Before the discussion of the
rules was over in London, however, some of the
dribbling players at Cambridge had also elected
a committee and drawn up a set of rules upon
which the old players of Eton, Harrow, Westminster and Charterhouse could agree. The Cambridge rules naturally excluded all running with
the ball, and the "hacking over", "tripping" and
"tackling" which were the means used by the
Rugbeians to stop the runners. The next move
was a joint conference of the London and Cambridge committees, and the dribbling players of
the metropolis naturally cast their vote against
the running and tackling which they reluctantly
inserted in their draft of rules in order to concili-
ate the London players of the Rugby game. The
result was that the combined influence of the
Cambridge and London dribblers was too strong
for the London Rugbeians, who accordingly
withdrew from the new combination which
started in 1863 under the name of the Football
Association, and has since worthily governed the
dribbling game. Even from its formation, however, the question of how to deal with the off-side
rule proved a stumbling block in the way of the
Association. The Etonians in playing their field
game had a rigorous rule against "sneaking" or

playing off-side, and the Harrovians also favoured a strict "off-side" rule. The Westminster
and Charterhouse boys, however, always played
the game of "passing forward", and were not in
favour of a strict off-side rule.

For the time the Etonians had their way, and
it was not until 1867 that the Association
adopted its present off-side rule, which provides
that no man can be "off-side" unless there are
less than three players of the opposite side in
front of him when the ball is passed. The Sheffield Association, a body of associated clubs who
played in the Sheffield district, went even further than the Association in their off-side rule,
and only obliged one opponent to be between the
players and the goal to prevent off- side play. For
the next ten years the Sheffielders played a
different game from the Londoners, until they at
length succumbed to the increasing power of the
Association, and adopted the prevalent rule.

It is from about this time only that football
has really become a national game, known
throughout the country. Most of the provincial
clubs playing under either set of rules have been
established since that date. The first international match between England and Scotland
under Association rules was played in 1872. For
the last dozen years the popularity of the game,
both with players and with spectators, has

spread marvellously, until at the time of writing football is as much the national game of winter as cricket is of summer. If antiquity of origin is to be considered as constituting an additional claim to honour, the game the history of which we have chronicled in this chapter stands pre-eminent amongst English sports.

Athletics and Football, 1887

Sir Montague Shearman (1857-1930) was a barrister, athlete and footballer. He co-founded the Amateur Athletics Association, and was a member of the Wanderers football club. His legal career was cut short by an illness related to an injury he suffered playing football. This article is an edited extract from Athletics and Football, his important 1887 text, which was republished in five editions, and is referenced in many subsequent football histories.

*"The clever footballer
is a celebrity."*

A Football Match

From a Correspondent, 1892

~

TO those of us who are accustomed to open
spaces it seems a wretched little enclosure, this
football ground in a great northern town. It is
surrounded by a high black fence, and houses
almost as black overlook it on all sides. The
ground itself is well adapted for play, but the
space between the ropes and the fence is so narrow that the modest little pavilion seems to be
all frontage, as if the plans for the complete
building had been lost; and elsewhere there is
scarcely room for the spectators to move about,
for an important League match is to be played,
and there must be quite eight or ten thousand
people present. They are evidently very well
pleased with the ground, for you may hear who
that are strange to it remark, "Eh, lad, but it's a
bonnie ground." Moreover, they have not come
with the intention of being listless onlookers.
Every man has his own opinion as to how the
game will go, and what is more, is prepared to
"back" it. One thinks "Jock" is a little stale, and

will be unable to stop the rush of the opposing forwards, while another declares that "Sandy" will make mincemeat of them, and that "Tim" will be "all there" in goal. Withal, it is a good-humoured and well-behaved crowd. All this goes on while a few of the players are attempting to shoot impossible goals and otherwise warming themselves for the contest.

But the spirit of speculation and prophecy is suddenly checked, for the sides have taken their places, and, in perfect quietude, the centre forward starts the ball. And now one has a good opportunity to admire the players themselves. There is nothing like uniformity amongst them. Some are tall, and others short, and one or two are somewhat bandy-legged, but it is at once clear that they are in splendid condition and fully capable of lasting through the heavy work which is expected from them in the next hour and a half. For the most part they are Scotchmen who look at the game seriously, as Scotchmen look at things in general. However, "the play's the thing", and we must imitate the crowd, and, indebted to their enthusiasm, follow the game closely. Centre forward passes the ball gently to the inside man on the right wing, who kicks it to his colleagues on the opposite sides of the ground, much to the surprise of his opponents, who are not quite prepared for this sudden development. The left wing men immediately get "on" the ball, and the excitement at once begins, for by clever combined play they elude the half-backs, and then place the ball at the feet of their centre, who is well forward, and immediately shoots at goal. The shot is fast and well judged, but the ball grazes the post and goes out of play. This early and brilliant attack thoroughly arouses the spectators, who shout their congratulations to the individuals, and in voices of thunder exhort the men generally to "play up". One of the backs "takes the kick", and the scene is changed to the other end of the field, where the goalkeeper only manages to prevent the forwards from scoring by knocking the ball behind the goal-line, and so giving the other side a "corner". It is interesting to observe how the defenders arrange their forces in order to avert the serious danger which threatens. Every man is in his place—the back division close in to goal, and the forwards prepared for a dash to the other end of the ground. One of the half-backs on the attacking side takes his place at the corner, and favoured by the urgent advice of the spectators, or in spite of it, he kicks so successfully that the ball falls in the mouth of the goal. Like a piece of animated indiarubber a figure bounds up, receives the ball on its head, and returns into play, where it is pounced upon, and, the ground being quite clear except for the backs, carried to the opposite goal. Almost before the side realises that it has relieved itself from immediate danger it finds that a goal has been scored—in its favour. The spectators, or sections of them, become wild with delight. Hats are thrown in the air, sticks are flourished, and the partisans of the two teams enter into a noisy rivalry in appealing to their favourites.

And so the game proceeds for three-quarters of an hour, at which time the teams change ends and the struggle is renewed. Even if you are ignorant of the rules of football, you cannot help admiring the skill and coolness of the players. Every man is a sprinter, and he moves so easily that, seen over the heads of other spectators, he appears to be gliding along without the slightest effort. Look, too, at the calm and deliberate play of the forwards. Only a few years ago the ideal forward was a man who dashed through his opponents with the chance of getting a goal or a broken leg. Such play was often exciting, and when exhibited by a man like [Nevill "Nuts"] Cobbold, brilliant in the extreme; but if a "professional" attempted it at the present time he would be bowled off any northern ground. An infinitely better method has been devised. Instead of clinging to the ball in the face of obstacles which cannot be overcome, the modern

forward passes it to his colleagues with a clear
run before them; and in this way the game has
been made more scientific and less dangerous,
since collisions are not so frequent. Here is a
man, for instance, who finds himself confronted
by a pair of half-backs, who are prepared to
defeat nay forward movement he may make. He
knows that he cannot hope to pass these alert
opponents, and, after a little manoeuvring, in the
course of which he has been looking for an
opening on the other wing, and at the same time
watching the men in front of him, he sends the
ball back towards his own goal. He has seen that
he might make a mistake by passing to the other
wing, and he prefers to give his half-backs the
opportunity of placing the ball where there is the
best opening for a run. Unless a man can play
with this coolness and judgement, he is quite
useless for modern high-class football. See,
moreover, the combined keenness and caution
with which the backs await the development of a
determined attack. Down come the opposing
forwards in a line stretching across the ground.
Without checking their speed, they pass and
repass the ball, and gradually close in towards
the goal. Meanwhile, the defending backs, with
bent heads and straining muscles, follow every
movement, and, heedless of the roaring crowd,
slowly retreat until the moment for action shall

arrive. Presently, one of the forwards slightly overkicks the ball, and, like a flash of lightning, the back darts out, and in an instant the play is transferred to the centre of the ground.

Nobody who witnesses a match between two first-class teams can wonder at the hold football has obtained upon the affections of the people, and few would go away without having suddenly acquired an interest in the game. Changes in the fortunes of the players occur every moment. Within a minute of the goal at one end being threatened the goalkeeper at the other end may be called to resist an attack. The ball constantly travels up and down the ground, and at every stage the onlookers see something to admire in the courage or skill of certain players. There is no other game which is capable of producing the eagerness and excitement that are noticeable at every good football match, and there is no other which brings into equal prominence the merits of individuals. Contrast all the excitement with the sedate interest aroused by a three days' cricket match, and the secret of the popularity of football becomes evident. The winter game brings every heroic quality into play, and it is well worthy to share with cricket the honour of being termed one of our two national games.

Daily News, 15 October 1892 (and syndicated)

Latter-Day Football

A Crude Critic, 1888

~

FOOTBALL is not what it used to be. It has
improved in many ways in recent years, both in
itself and in its hold on the public. It is a far
more scientific game than it was, say, half a
dozen years ago. The ball used to be regarded as
a hardly-treated article which got about the field
rather by accident than by design, whereas
nowadays the steps that have animated its direction are keenly watched as means to an end, and
are easily intelligible as such. The game itself is
not, perhaps, quite as rough as it was. In the
Association game, mark the self-possession of the
"field" as compared with the flurry of former
days. Every one, from the forward dribbler, curl-
ing and twisting the leather, which seems to
adapt itself knowingly to every movement of his
feet, to the goalkeepers, almost out of "covey",
but who knows by experience that "them things
as seems least likelier than them as seems most
likeliest" is on the alert, excited, perhaps, with
the chops and changes in the game, but, above

all, wary and contained. There is little aimless rushing hither and thither. When collisions occur they seem the necessary outcome of an organised plan. This is certainly more agreeable to the eye than the "do or die" rushes which produced much damage to the human body vile with the minimum of result on the course of the game; and we may reasonably suppose it to be far more satisfactory to the players themselves. So highly developed is football not that, to a spectator, the interest is quite as much in the head as in the leg work. To look at any of our celebrated teams or footballers it is evident that each player regards himself as only a unit in a combination, with a definite part to play. He has the measure of the capacities of each member of his own side, and regulates his play with reference quite as much to their anticipated share in the game as to his own individual prowess. If there are fewer kicks now in the football field, there are more, far more, halfpence to be picked up there. A few years ago professionalism in football was as unknown as is a decent four-wheel cab at the present day; but now it is an invidious task to say which of our great football teams is not professional all through. The trail of the pot-hunter and the money-grubber is over the game. "It stinks o' brass," as the Manchester millionaire [Samuel Brooks] affectionately said of himself.

The football club is no longer a congeries of men and boys, with a ball for their capital and a desire for an hour's fun for their object. It must be started and advertised like a limited liability company, with influential names and a heavy subscription list. Practised agents must be employed to scout the kingdom for recruits. If a good man from a distance cannot be induced to attach himself to the fortunes of a club by change of residence without an exceptionally liberal offer, the offer must be made. If he is famous, and has to be detached from the interests of another club, the terms for a transference of his allegiance are pretty much what he chooses to make them. His chances of money-making are by no means exhausted by the regular receipt of a comfortable income. In the North and in the Midlands particularly footballers carry a good deal of the public money; and appreciative winners are apt to be generous to the players who have helped to line their pockets. Then there are nice pickings from the "gate" and prospective "benefits", to say nothing of the money value of the high social estimation in which footballers of renown are held. It is a privilege worth paying for to be permitted to photograph these gentlemen; while to supply them with soap, pills, restoratives, laxatives, wine, groceries, and other *deliciae vitae,* free of cost in consideration of an

THE DRIBBLING GAME

acknowledgement by the recipients of the supreme value of these articles, is a mode of advertisement not altogether unknown. The clever footballer is a celebrity in the Northern and Midland counties. That is the long and short of the matter. It may be right, or it may be wrong, that he should be so, and that he should turn his position to making the best pecuniary advantage for himself out of it. As to that I say nothing. Let wiser critics decide. There is at least to be said, that professionalism has improved football, whatever may be the effect it has had on the votaries of the game. More than that, it has made the game enormously popular.

Pall Mall Gazette, 25 February 1888

Making a Big Football Club

Frank Brettell and the Hotspurs
Henry Leach, 1898

~

A FEW, but only a few, may wonder who Mr. Brettell is. To most readers he will be known as the new secretary and manager of the Tottenham Hotspur Football Club, which has embarked upon an enterprise of a most daring and important character. The shortest and simplest way of explaining the nature of that enterprise is by saying that the Hotspur Club aims at becoming, and is determined to become, one of the biggest clubs in the country all at once.

Now, feeling very sure that here was a subject which would very much interest the readers of this paper, one day not long ago I made tracks for Northumberland Park, where the Hotspurs play, and after seeing them gain two United League points at the expense of Luton I followed Mr. Brettell to the club office, where, busy as he was, he told me the whole story.

Just glance at first at what the Hotspurs have been, and are. Till recently they were quite a humble lot, comparatively, not having the assurance to consider themselves in the same class as the big League clubs of the Midlands and the North. Now they, Southampton, and one or two others, are leading the way in a revival of the South. They are a professional club; they have turned themselves, according to the custom of big clubs, into a limited liability company, with a capital of £8,000; they have engaged, at a big salary, a real live First League secretary to look after and manage the club, and they have induced many real live First League players to come and win their matches for them. So, as our Yankee cousins would say, the Tottenham Hotspurs mean "getting there".

The First League secretary I have just alluded to is, of course, Mr. F. E. Brettell, and I asked him first of all to tell me something about himself, who he was, where he came from, and so on. Certainly what Mr. Brettell does not know about football cannot be worth knowing, for he has been connected with the game in almost every possible capacity during a period of twenty years. He was among those who formed the original Everton Club, now one of the wealthiest and most famous in England. He became secretary of it and was a most enthusiastic player, but very unlucky. Once he had his chest smashed in, and another time one of his legs went with a crack

MR. F. E. BRETTELL

which could be heard all over the ground; so that among the penalties he has had to pay for his love of the game has been several months' occupation of a hospital bed. He was originally a forward, playing centre and inside left, but in his latter days he figured at half-back and sometimes in goal.

Later on he was the special football representative of a Liverpool newspaper, and becoming connected with the Liverpool club, he was given charge of the team at a critical period in its history, before the redoubtable Tom Watson took the red-shirted boys in hand.

Then he became secretary of the Bolton Wanderers, another big League club. That was about three years ago.

"I heard the Wanderers wanted a new secretary," he said, "but I never thought about putting in for it until my friends told me I ought to do so. I obtained strong recommendations from Mr. J. J. [John James] Bentley, the president of the League, and Mr. [John] Lewis, both names to conjure with in the football world, and though there were ninety-eight applications—I know this because I had to answer them all afterwards—I was one of three selected for an interview. In the waiting-room I met one of the other two, who was an old friend of mine from the North. It was rather awkward. A local candidate was strongly in the running; but the committee declared they liked my views of management and training, and all that sort of thing, and I was engaged."

Now he has come to Tottenham, and you know what sort of man he is who has been entrusted to the task of making a big football club.

"Well, what have you been doing? How have you been going about it?" I asked.

"The first thing to do was to get good men," was the reply. "For our purposes it would not do to engage doubtful ones and trust to them turning out well. We had to get the ready-made article, the very best League players from the very best clubs, and had to pay them their price. We have got some internationals—[Tom] Bradshaw, the famous Liverpool left-winger, for instance, who has twice played for England against Ireland."

It will be interesting for you to note that, though Mr. Brettell believed in getting tried men for his team, he has great ideas about discovering likely youngsters, and he told me that he would only be too glad to meet by appointment any young player who wished to join them, and give them a trial. So there's a chance for you youngsters! If he can get hold of enough of them he plans to put a whole team of juniors of this sort against another team of them, and then watch them carefully. He told me about some of the talent he has assisted to unearth.

"Bradshaw, one of the best forwards in England, is a sample," he said. "He was secured seven years ago. First, he was quite a lad in short knickerbockers, playing for the Lansdowne club in Stanley Park, Liverpool. Someone noticed him; and Liverpool and Everton were advised to try him, but they would not hear of it. On the advice of another well-known player, Fred Geary of Everton, he went to Northwich Victoria, and while he was playing there among others I noticed him and at once advised Liverpool to take both him and another one, and after some bother he was tried in a match at Plumstead. He at once became a regular member of the team.

"Now, here is the story of a queer catch I made, and a rare good one, too. A couple of seasons ago something went wrong with [John Willie] Sutcliffe, the famous Bolton goal-keeper—a muscle of the leg was strained—so I took him over to Manchester to see Dr. Whitehead, the specialist, who has a little football hospital there. Dr. Whitehead being engaged until the evening, I had nothing particularly to do, so I walked about. A poster advertising a small match caught my eye, and I said to myself, 'I will go and see what there is to be seen.' I saw something. A young lad named [John] Fitchett was playing in one of the teams, and the match hadn't been going on for long before I had the sort of feeling that I had 'struck oil'. Fitchett impressed me so much that I went specially to see him play again. Manchester City were his opponents this time, and he played a great game against a very formidable opposition.

"I made up my mind we must get him, so I took a strong team of Bolton Wanderers to play his club West Manchester, and afterwards I saw his father. I worked the trick—well, never mind how. I asked him as a favour to let his lad come and help us in the last match of the season. Consent was given, and though Fitchett junior was only a lad of seventeen—5 feet 10 inches in height, though—he did splendidly. Sutcliffe and Jones, two of our men, said he was the most promising youngster they ever put eyes on. He played for us the next season as an amateur; but I found that other clubs were after him, so at length I persuaded him to sign a League form and turn professional, which secured him for us. He is doing very well as a half-back for Bolton now. I came across another lad named Hallowes in a very similar way. We took him off the pit bank."

"While we are on this subject Mr. Brettell, can't you give some advice to young footballers who wish to become first-class players?"

"Yes; and I give them the same advice as poor 'Nick' Ross gave to his brother Jimmy. Nicholas John Ross—he was always called Nick for short—was one of the finest backs who have ever lived, and belonged to Preston North End when it carried all before it. He is dead now, poor fellow.

"Well, his brother Jimmy came to Lancashire with the idea of playing regularly, and being a youngster, knew very little about the game. This is 'Nick's' own tale. So 'Nick' took him in hand, and determined to make a player of him. Young James, only a lad then, was taken out regularly by his brother, and was first set to practicing sprinting and running with the ball, till by the by he became one of the fasters sprinters and dribblers and best shots that have ever been seen. He was taught how to gain immediate control over the ball when it came to him from all conceivable angles, and how to part with it at once. Those are great points, and he was taught them one by one by a great master.

"If there is one thing which a player is poor at—say centring the ball on the run—he should practise that and nothing else till he is quite perfect. That is what Jimmy did, and then he was set to practise and play with the North End forwards—[Jack] Gordon, [John] Goodall, [Sam] Thompson, [Fred] Dewhurst, and [Geordie]

Drummond—the finest line that has ever stepped on to a field. He became the most brilliant man of the lot. A striking feature of his play is his wonderful finish. For thirty yards he would beat any man. He is playing for Burnley now."

"Then I take it that you consider that any player can make himself a first-class player without being born one?"

Well, of course, you know some show greater adaptability to the game than others, and that goes a long way; but anyone who has really got the will can make himself a pretty good player. He must practise at his weak points. A full back, perhaps, cannot take a 'punt'; give him punts till he can. A goal-keeper who is weak at low shots should have low shots banged into him till he likes them. To become a brilliant player you must bestow earnest application and attention to the practice games.

"I might just say that I don't believe in doing any 'special training' at all. My advice to a player in that respect is to lead a simple, plain, and steady life, and not to neglect his ordinary work, but keep to it, and practise in the evenings once or twice a week. Then the game becomes a real recreation to him and not a bore, and he keeps in much better health. I always try to get work for any players who wish it."

Reverting again to the Hotspurs, Mr. Brettell

told me they had every confidence of success all year round. As for the "sinews of war", he said that in its amateur days the club drew about £500 in a season in gate money. Last year the amount received was over £4,000. "It is a very big organisation which is being developed here," he said.

Football, he believes, is coming down South altogether; and no matter what success they achieve, the Hotspurs will stick to the Southern League, which Mr. Brettell thinks will be equal to *the* League in the near future.

Chums, 19 October 1898

Frank Brettell was a player and secretary for St Domingo, the Methodist Church team that, in 1879, became Everton FC. As club secretary, he was responsible for the running of the club, and was effectively Everton's first manager. He was also a football reporter for the Liverpool Mercury. After injury halted his playing career, he moved to Bolton as secretary, and then to Tottenham. He was at Spurs for less than a year, moving to Portsmouth, and then Plymouth Argyle. At the time of this interview, Tottenham were competing in both the Southern League and the short-lived United League. They were elected to the second division of the Football League in 1908.

Opening the Season

A Special Correspondent, 1898

~

BEFORE some of us have quite realised that there has been a season of the year called summer, the date on which partridge shooting and football begin has come and gone. The glories of cricket have faded away temporarily, for nobody takes much interest much interest in the holiday games at the seaside, and public attention is ardently turned to the great winter pastime.

There is no question of the eagerness with which the change has been welcomed. Folks are football mad already. When they cannot watch their favourite entertainment given in earnest, they are content with the rehearsals. Whoever heard of people turning up in thousands to witness practice games at any other outdoor sport? Nobody, of course. But your football enthusiast will go night after night to watch his pet football team getting into condition. For one thing, he has not to pay for the treat; and we all know, almost as well as theatrical managers, how attractive free admissions are.

THE FOOTBALLER'S HOLIDAY

This football practice is a serious business—a very serious business in Association circles. A short consideration will prove its importance. At the end of April last the professional football finished a period of eight months' hard labour. During this spell he had to exercise so much self-denial, to enter into a vast amount of violent exertion, and to deprive himself of many of the social joys which he loves. With the end of April came the end of his labours. He had before him, for three months at any rate, unreserved liberty, out of sight and out of the authority of trainers and committees. And he at once set about enjoying himself in his own way.

Some of the men, no doubt, keep in condition all the year round. Indeed, we have heard this week of a famous international who has go to loggerheads with his committee already because he has preferred playing in second-class county cricket up until the end of August rather than practice football. But the majority of professional footballers, I am afraid, do nothing so sensible as cricket in the summer. They give themselves up to lounging and excessive eating, not to mention excessive drinking. After their eight months of toil they feel entitled to have their fling. The consequence is that they get as fat as bullocks

GIVE THEMSELVES UP TO LOUNGING

which are in preparation for the dead-meat market, and almost as scant of breath as the average Manchester man who never does anything much more violent than chase a tramcar for a score or two of yards.

GETTING INTO FORM

When they turn up for their first practice their trainer knows exactly what he has to do. He must reduce their bulk pretty considerably, and he does it by arranging a severe course of training under the hot August sun. For a time the diminishing person operated upon feels that life is not worth living. He is possessed by yearnings, almost irresistible, to give up the game. But he cannot afford that, and after a time, as his *avoirdupois*[9] becomes more and more limited, his views change. He begins to delight in his work. He faintly resembles, in some of his movements, the lambs as they were six months ago. Visions of the great feats he will perform before admiring thousands enter into his head, and he grows almost as eager for the beginning of the eight months' struggle as his committee are for the arrival of the day on which they can replenish exhausted exchequers by heaps of gate money.

---

[9] Body of weight (Middle English).

To this stage we have already arrived. Indeed, some clubs have passed it, for one or two games were played last night.

THE ABOLITION OF THE TEST GAMES

The practice games are of the first importance, for the reason that the serious business begins straight away. Upon a goal or two, scored or failed to be scored, in the earliest matches, the most momentous issue may depend at the close of the season. Take as an example the case of a club in the First Division of the Association League. Not one of them escapes the ordeal of playing for its position. There are eighteen organisations, two in excess of the number of last year, of whom everyone meets all the others in two encounters. The two clubs at the bottom of the list at the close of the season lose their places. They are relegated automatically to the Second Division of the League. This deposition carried in its train terrible consequences. The deposed club no longer has visits on alternate Saturdays from the famous organisations whose names are household words throughout the north of England. In their place come second-rate elevens, who are not nearly so good a draw. The "gates" inevitable suffer, and all the word becomes dark.

Since last season the process of deposing two clubs from the First Division, and promoting two clubs from the Second Division to take their place, has undergone a notable change. Fortunately the last two clubs in the senior branch had to play test games with the two top teams in the second branch, and on the result of these games depended the location of the clubs for the season. To avoid the test matches was the object of every organisation, and many curious stories are told of the means to secure this end. Tactics that were not at all fair were often introduced. We all remember how, a season or two ago, a well-known club needed to beat another eleven, considerably its superior, by six goals to nothing, to avoid the tests, and how it just managed to accomplish the feat. Nobody ever believed that it could have won by the desired margin without the connivance of its alleged opponents. Another device which there is reason to believe has been resorted to is known in football circles as squaring the referee. It is so easy for the ruler of the game for the time being to declare that goals scored by a side which does not want to win are off-side.

ASSOCIATION CLUBS IN MANCHESTER

Scandals of this character have had much to do

with the abolition of the test games. In future the two bottom teams in the First Division will be relegated to the Second Division, and the two top teams in the Second Division will be promoted to the First Division without a contest of any sort. The change is charged with pleasing possibilities for the growing numbers who follow Association football in the Manchester district. We have, in our city, two clubs who have generally succeeded in getting a prominent position in the Second Division. If they have not been at the top they have been near the top. Now a determined effort will be made to attain the position which will enable them, without more ado, to step into the senior division.

It has long been my opinion, in Association circles in Manchester, that it is something of a reflection on our character as "football sports" that we have not had, except for one brief season, a First League team in the city. Everyone is aware that our two leading clubs have an enormous following, that the crowds who watch their performances are gigantic, and that the amount that is paid as gate-money reaches a colossal figure, a figure higher than many organisations who have had a place in the front ranks through many seasons. Then the fact is pointed out that towns like Sheffield and Nottingham can run two first-class teams, and that Liverpool, which is not held to be as big a sporting centre as Manchester, has also two elevens. How comes it, then, that Newton Heath and City have been in the second string so long? "Because they were not good enough to go higher," is the obvious answer. The query "why are they not good enough" is more difficult to reply to. The directors of the two combinations claim that they have done their best to get together the strongest elevens that they could command, and assert that ill-luck has had something to do with their want of success in the past.

THE CONFIDENT SECRETARY AND THE GUILELESS JOURNALIST

What about the future? The wise man accepts prophecies on football matters with the utmost reluctance. He knows that they cannot be trusted. At the beginning of the football season every football secretary in the land assumes, if he does not feel, an air of perfect confidence. When the simple-minded journalist, like myself, goes to him with a polite inquiry about his club's prospects he positively beams. "My boy," he says—they have a way of beginning with my boy—"we have a lot better than me have ever had. Our men will astonish you this year. They have never done as well as they will do this season, mark my

GETTING INTO CONDITION

words." The first time one hears this he is impressed. The second time the impression is not quite worn off, but when the tale is repeated at the beginning of every year by nearly every secretary one meets, even the most guileless of journalists is apt to lighten up his features with the smile of incredulity. "The wish is father to the prophecy," he mutters, and turns sceptically away.

The reader of the foregoing paragraph will not need to be told why the writer of this article gives no glowing account of the prospects of either City or Newton Heath, preferring the safer course of allowing his readers to judge of their chances of joining the senior division after they have played a few matches.

To-morrow the game will begin in real earnest. Very hot work it will prove, and there will be much larding of the lean earth. Let us hope that, learning lessons from the past, the men will make an endeavour to play the game good temperedly. Then, though there will be accidents, as there always have been and always will be in a hard game like football, there will be nothing serious to complain about. It will be a sad day for the English youth when he becomes afraid of running the risk of getting a knock or two.

Manchester Times, 2 September 1898

Association Football in Scotland

David Drummond Bone, 1880

~

BOTH Association and Rugby Football seem to come to the Scotchmen by nature. The history of Association Football, with which I have only to deal under the present circumstances, is well-known (or should be known) to all who take an interest in the game. In my previous article in The Annual I tried to trace the origin of football in its rudest form as played by our forefathers, when goal-posts and bars, to say nothing of corner-flags, were unknown. Football now, however, has been reduced to something like a scientific game, and to the credit of England be it said, the Association Rules there first saw the light. Scotch players in the Western District soon emulated their Southern brethren, and from the parent club, which had a humble and unassuming origin on the recreation ground at Queen's Park, sprang hundreds of clubs, spreading over the length and breadth of the land with remarkable rapidity. The wave soon rolled all over Glasgow and suburbs, submerged the whole country, and eventually invaded the Heart of Midlothian itself, where the Rugby code had hitherto reigned supreme. The schoolboys who played cricket and "rounders" in the summertime came out on a wintry afternoon to see their seniors engaged in Association football, and soon felt the desire creep over them to be members of a club containing lads like themselves. The young men engaged in the city all day thought on the health-imparting exercise it afforded, and had the necessary funds raised to form a club. The artisans, too, from the dusky foundry, the engineer shop, and the factory, soon began to dribble about. The young ones, and even the seniors themselves, had many a collision with mother earth ere they could rely on keeping their pins with any degree of accuracy, and it was rare fun to see a bearded man turning a somersault as he missed the ball in trying to make a big kick.

Football is easily acquired in so far as the rudimentary part is concerned, but a great deal of probation is required to convert one into a crack player. Among those who now practice football, and their name is legion, the superior players can be numbered in (to give it a wide scope) hundreds. In fact, to be able to master all the details requisite to win a first-class match, one has to be capable of dribbling, middling, heading, and passing in a way that would do credit to solving a complicated problem in Euclid. It is all very well to talk about brute force and lasting power, but unless these are accompanied by scientific application, they are worth little, and cost much. "The race is not always to the swift," says the old proverb. In at least eight cases out of ten, the match is to the scientific and careful, but of this more anon.

There is one thing that can be said about football which in the nature of things must recommend it to all lovers of out-door exercise. Of late years bicycling has obtained a great deal of popularity all over the three kingdoms, both for its usefulness as a speedy means of conveyance, and exercise to the limbs, but that it has its drawbacks has just been made apparent by undisputed medical authority. "The bicycle back", the effect of hard work on the "iron horse", is beginning to appear on the handsome young man who thinks nothing of doing his 50 miles a day, and while walking occasionally with the young lady with the "Grecian bend",[10] the contrast in his case is amusing. To say that there are no dangers of any kind attached to football would be making an assertion which I cannot substantiate, but these are comparatively few. All sports, of whatever kind, have the elements of danger

---

[10] Female stoop created by fashion for corsets and bustles.

attached to their pursuit, but, with great care, these can be reduced to a minimum. Although I have certainly never observed the round-shoulders of the bicyclist in the football player, I have not unfrequently seen the "football leg". That is a series of cuts about the shin bone, administered by a vicious opponent while (as it generally happens) playing a "cup tie", and last season they were more plentiful than ever. In fact, I heard from the lips of a member of one of the crack clubs that in not a few of the ties they retired from the field "greatly impressed with the unmistakable signs of muscular ability shown by their opponents." This means most undoubtedly hacking and tripping, under the guise of tackling, and if Association football is to go on and prosper such disgraceful acts of tyranny on the football field must forever cease. These "accidents" can, of course, be avoided, and as there are distinct rules forbidding them, clubs would do well to see that these are rigidly enforced.

Spectators and patrons are to be found in all ranks and conditions of life, from the lord of the manor down to the apprentice artisan and newly-fledged young man from the shop and warehouse. Like love, football for the time, at least, levels all distinctions, and albeit I know, for that of it, many a well-matched pair, who have met for the first time on the grand stand at Hampden

Park, looking back with feelings of intense pleasure to a time when their "infant love began". Were it not, in fact, that Caledonia is at times so "stern and wild", and that football and frost can never flourish together, the game would be far more extensively patronised by the fair sex. At a Cup tie or an international match it is quite a common thing to see the Convener of an adjacent county, the city magnate, the suburban magistrate, the Free Kirk minister, and the handsome matronly lady standing side by side with the horny-handed mechanic, the office boy, the overgrown schoolboy, and the Buchanan Street "swell". They all watch the game and surroundings in their own particular way.

As the Association Rules are very easily learned in theory, the great bulk of the spectators show an acquaintance with them which is pleasing to see, and when an assumed infringement takes place it is generally heralded from some part of the field by a partisan of the contending elevens. The only apparently unintelligible point to them is the "off-side" rule, and I have seen a goal kicked in this way hailed with deafening cheers and waving of hats and handkerchiefs. These manifestations, however, were turned into low moaning when the leather was sent away by a free kick. The ladies, too, talk about "free kicks", "corner-kicks", "heading", "hands", "beautiful passing and dribbling", as if to the manor born. I cannot, however, dismiss the subject of spectators without referring to the use and abuse of a free and unrestrained vent to pent-up feelings. There is the low, vulgar fellow, whose collarless neck and general coarseness of exterior and language indicates that he possesses all the vices but none of the virtues of the "honest working man". Work he will not, except he is compelled, and although to "beg he is ashamed", he would be the first to do a mean action if he had the opportunity. It is he who, by his foul tongue and very breath, contaminates the atmosphere he breathes, and brings some of the matches into disrepute. Unfortunately he has paid his money at the gate (sometimes he gets over the fence), and you can't turn him out; but he makes hundreds miserable. He is, in fact, one of the "unimproving and irresponsible", and moral suasion has no power over his hard and stony heart. Sometimes in an evil moment his vulgar remark is challenged by one of the players on the contending sides, and this gives him an air of importance. There is nothing, however, which shows a want of gentlemanly bearing in a team more clearly than paying the least attention to exclamations from excited spectators. They should treat them with silent indifference, and if needs be, contempt, and play away

as if there were nobody present at all. It is sometimes, nevertheless, very hard for country clubs
to come to Glasgow and play for the city chari-
ties, and get howled at by this class of spectators
at certain stages of the game. The great bulk of
those around, however, are indignant at such
conduct, and regret it all the more on account of
being utterly unable to prevent it.

There is another spectator, too, who not unfrequently forgets himself, and he is to be found
on what might be termed the "touch-line" of
society. He is the fast young man, who considers
you a perfect nonentity if you don't bet. I don't
mean betting on football pure and simple, for he
only lays a few "bobs" on it, but on the latest
quotations for the Derby, the St. Leger, the Waterloo Cup, or the University Boat Race. His
"screw" is not very big at the best, but he can
always lay "half a sov." on the event, whether his
landlady's bill is paid or not, and touching that
little account of Mr. Strides, the tailor, why, he'll
pay it when he "makes a pile". He thinks too
much of himself ever to get married, and the
young ladies of his acquaintance may indulge in
a sigh of relief at escaping from the toils of such
a consummate fool. When he has something "on"
a match, and sees that it is lost, he not unfrequently opens out, and is not over choice in his
language. The game, however, goes on, and is

greatly enjoyed by the general spectator, despite such drawbacks, and if you happen to go to the same locality on a similar occasion, you are all but sure to see old and familiar faces crowding round the stand and area.

Shall Association Football eventually die out in Scotland? When the summer game of cricket was far more extensively played in Glasgow and District than it is now, those who understood the feelings and aspirations of young men engaged in it repeatedly considered the question in all its aspects, and a combination of circumstances have occurred within the last decade which had seriously affected that game. The City of Glasgow could not, of course, afford to remain in a stationary condition to suit the convenience of a few thousands of cricketers. New streets had to be formed, new houses built all round, and with this advance upon civilisation came the deadly blow to cricket—at least juvenile cricket—and those clubs soon disappeared from the field. Ground after ground was swallowed up, and on the scene of many a hot and exciting match blocks of houses, railway stations, churches, and public works may now be seen. The Scotch youth, and for that part of it (just to give the sentence greater weight), the British youth, loves some kind of manly sport. Cricket he could no longer play for want of good and level ground, but then there was another game which, at least, could be played or learned under easy circumstances, even on a quiet street or big "free coup", and that was Association football. They soon took to it kindly, and many of them struggled hard and procured a ground. Not one, of course, like that on which they used to have their cricket matches long ago, but one on which Farmer Lyon grazed his cows and sheep, and they had it for a trifle. What did they care about ridges and furrows, or that it was a difficult matter to see the lower goal-posts when you were at the east end? Not a straw. The only matter which annoyed them (and this only happened occasionally) was Lyon's bull. Their club colours were red jerseys, with a small white stripe, and "Jock" (that was the animal's name), used to scatter the lads about on the Friday evenings when they were engaged in a big side. The players generally managed to clear out in time, but the infuriated animal once goared the best ball the club had, and next morning, as they had to play the "Invincible" of Glasgow Green, a subscription had to be raised for a new one.

Football can thus be played under much more favourable conditions than cricket, or almost any other out-door game, at less expense, and this, in a great measure at least, is the secret of its popularity amongst the masses. It can also be played under nearly every condition of the atmosphere. Nothing seems to frighten the Scotch Association football player. Rain, hail, snow, and even frost, is treated with cool indifference. In England the ball is quietly laid aside with the advent of April and forgotten till the Autumn leaves are yellow and sear, but in Scotland Association football seems to have no recognised season at all, so far as the younger clubs and even a few of the seniors are concerned. With the sun making one's hair stick to his head with perspiration, and the thermometer at 95 degrees in the shade, they play away in the summer-time, and at Christmas attempt to dribble in half-a-foot of snow.

Meantime the question about football being blotted out can, I think, be easily answered in the negative, and upon these will depend the future prospect of Association Football in Scotland. There are, in fact, "breakers ahead", and a strong and determined hand will have to take the wheel. The greatest of these is the "professional" football player, and the next the "greed of gate-money". "O! We never heard of a professional football player in Scotland," exclaims a chorus of voices; "there is no such thing. It's only in England." My remark, of course, is only beginning to be realised. The definition of professional in athletics "is one who runs (plays) for gain". Everybody knows what that means. If you receive any money whatever, directly or indirectly, from your club (except out of the private purses of the members), you are a professional. Are there not clubs, with great reputations, who have such members? If these are allowed to continue on the club books simply because they are good players, the committee are doing a great injustice to the other members, it may be under a mistaken notion. Now, as football has always been looked upon as a purely amateur game, and played by young men for their own amusement, it is to be hoped that the day is far distant when the professional football player, or even worse, the professional football "loafer", who does not work, but preys upon his fellow-members, will appear in a general form. In all conscience, if the public wish to see professional football (and I know from experience they don't), what would they think of the All-Scotland Eleven against the Champion Eleven of England? That might sound all right, but with the recollection of how professional athletics of all kinds (with the remarkable exception of cricket) are now conducted, and their low associations, woe betide football when the professional element is introduced. It will assuredly be the signal for its decline and fall.

As for the greed of gate-money, of which some clubs are so fond, much might be said. When I refer to the clubs who try to gather as much cash

as they can during the season in order to pay
their legitimate obligations and meet the heavy
item of ground rent, I show up an honourable
example, and one worthy of imitation; but when I
hear of clubs who have gathered ten, yea twenty
times more than is required for such purposes,
and even get handsome donations besides from
their patrons, deep in debt at the end of the
season, I begin to wonder where all the money
has gone. I ask a young gentleman who has only
lately become a member, and he tells me he
knows nothing about the finance committee, but
throws out grave hints about sordid motives and
bare-faced applications for pecuniary assistance.
In this respect clubs must be above suspicion, if
they want the delightful game to hold its own
and prosper. As a *quid pro quo* for this vicious
practice, however, there is no game whose players are so charitable as those connected with
Association Football. There is not a club in the
Association that is not ready to play a "Charity
Match," and far more has been given to the funds
of charitable institutions by the actions of Association football clubs than all the other games in
Scotland put together.

As has been illustrated over and over again in
all sublunary things, and assuredly football has
by no means exception, as the game increased in
public favour clubs began to get jealous of their

reputations. "Never to have been beaten," was a grand motto to be inscribed on their banner, but as others were slowly but surely approaching them in ability, how were they to maintain their position with becoming dignity?

A few years passed and found them still able to keep their own, but eventually it became a terrible struggle. Why, they practised as hard, if not harder than ever, the captain was certain, the forwards dribbled, passed, and backed up more brilliantly than before; the backs and half-backs tackled and kicked with as great a success against the second eleven as of yore, and the goalkeeper was ever on the ball when it came near, but, strange to say, they could not score anything like so many goals against their more powerful "opponents". What was the cause? Would none of the eleven dare to speculate? After a terrible tussle through a Cup tie, which had to be played three times before victory crowned their efforts by the narrow majority of one goal to nothing, the team had their eyes opened. One of the oldest dribblers remarked, "There isn't any disguising the fact; these fellow are fast gaining on us, and we'll soon get licked by our own chicks." This was quite true. Hundreds of clubs had started, and were practising the game with undaunted vigour, and it was only natural to suppose that many of them would soon come to the front. It was also admitted that the old club had lost none of their ability, but the young ones were fast approaching their standard, and as perfection is not of this earth, were determined at least to make a great effort to gain as many steps as they could on the ladder that led to its "sacred height". In this way club after club appeared on the field as each season came round, and in a terrible tussle on a bleak and rainy Saturday afternoon a persevering country club defeated those who has given them their first lesson in Association football. A question has often been asked—one really worth serious consideration of all players and devotees of the game—which might not only be legislated upon by a committee of clubs, but by the Scottish Football Association itself—"Is it fair for one club to reduce the power of another by inducing members to join its ranks?" Well, the question is a delicate one, and certain forms of it might be considered, to use a simile, like the suspension of the *Habeas Corpus* Act itself. In every game that I know of, particularly cricket, a sort of weakness exists amongst a certain class of players to be on the roll of the most successful club of the district and even the country itself, and they accordingly get admitted, play several matches, and sometimes make good scores; but beyond this the infatuation (if I may be pardoned for designating it as such) never goes, and they also do their best to make runs and bowl for their own club in many of its best matches. Unfortunately, however, such is not the case with football. The Association enacts that in playing "Cup ties" the member must select his club at the beginning of the season, and this is just and proper. Some might suggest that they should go a little further, and select the clubs that are to play for the trophy. Would that have the effect of checking the "drafting system"? Not at all. It must be left to the discretion of clubs who practise it, and the honour of individuals themselves. The most honourable way, however, is for clubs of standing to train their own players, and if the second and even third elevens are treated with a spirit of fairness there is not the least doubt about latent ability showing itself in a variety of ways, and while the gracious act will be all the more appreciated by younger members thus encouraged in well doing, football will be all the better for it.

The modern Association football player is a man of some ability. As a rule he is temperate in his habits, with a good appetite, and sound in limb. Long before he knew what football was, he was blessed with a large share of health. When a boy at school he used to be remarkable for punctuality, but occasionally got into trouble from neglected lessons, in consequence of a weakness for indulging in out-door sports. He loved the rude style of football, then played, dearly (he knew of nothing better), although goal-posts, touch-lines, corner-flags, and other modern appliances were totally unknown. As for "hacking", it was endured by all and sundry with the air of martyrs. Why, if you had not nerve enough to "give and take" in that line, your chance of getting near the "goal score" was remote indeed, and you were looked upon as a coward and the veriest noodle. He, of course, grows older, and by and by joins an average club, and gets on very well. The crack football players, however, have many maturities. They generally come slowly, but surely, and leave behind them powerful impressions. They are like the occasional planets, not the stars which are seen every evening if you care to look towards the "milky way". They are mostly fine-looking fellows, with pleasant countenances and grandly-moulded limbs. They have just passed a severe course of probation in the football field, without even an outward trace of anxiety. The vagaries of the game admit of no distinction of class. The crack player is, in fine, found among all classes—in the gentleman's son, in the clerk at the desk, and the lad in the workshop. There may be different ways of working out the latent ability, but sooner or later it begins to show itself. Some thought it was scarcely fair in

the Duke of Wellington to say that "Waterloo
was won at Eton". There is not the least possibil-
ity of doubt such a remark might be misunder-
stood, and many feel inclined to charge the "Iron
Duke" with ignoring the services rendered by the
non-commissioned officers and men of the British
army, for everybody knows that none but the
sons of the opulent class can ever gain admit-
tance to Eton. It looked, in fact, very like the
credit being given to the officers for winning that
great battle. Wellington, however, had his eye on
the football and cricket grounds when he spoke
these words, and no doubt intended to convey the
idea that these games went a long way in bracing
up the nerve which served so well on the battle
field. Close adhesion to the practice of any game
really and sincerely creates fresh possibilities of
that perfection and discipline. And why should
this not be so in football, particularly as it is a
game regulated by sharply-defined maxims?

Everyone can't be the captain of an eleven;
and as for Wellington's remarks, the most humble member of the team may show the greatest
ability. You may belong to the most "swellish" of
clubs, and have a fair reputation, but you are not
chosen to play in the International. Your father
may be the "Great Mogul" himself, but that has
no effect. The coveted place can only be attained
by merit, and this is one of the most successful

and meritorious traits in Scotch Association Football. You don't, as a rule, even get a place now by reputation, and so much the better. When clubs were few and good players fewer, you were not unfrequently favoured with one, whether you deserved it or not, but now the matter is different, and justly so, since we cannot go into a single town or village in Scotland without seeing the practice ground and goal-posts of the now omnipresent football club.

The successful player nowadays has many things to contend with. If he is a fine forward, and can dribble and dodge well, he has to guard against the opposing back or half-back. That "gentleman" may be what is vulgarly known as the "bully of the club" (some delight in keeping such). He "spots" the unfortunate dribbler as soon as the ball is kicked off, and "goes for him" on the earliest opportunity. What does the "bully" care about the opinion of spectators, or, for that part of it, the Association committee? They must win the Cup tie. Suppose they should send half their opponents to the "Western Infirmary". But even the "bully" can be done. As long kicking seems now to be universal amongst forwards (and this is to be regretted), let them come close to him, and whenever he charges like the infuriated bull, kick the leather over his head, and have one of your "backers-up" to follow. Charging opponents long before the ball comes near seems to be a favourite mode of procedure indulged in by many rough players nowadays. I would bring it under the notice of the Association, and insist on a remedy. Better to adopt the new rules of the Ayrshire Association, prohibiting charging under any circumstances, than run the chance of injured limbs; but I think the matter can be settled without that extreme measure. There is charging and charging. In all the course of my experience I have never seen a player hurt seriously in close tackling where the ball happened to be near. It is the cruel and deliberate charge which generally takes place in an attempt to get "on the ball" that causes the mischief, and the rule on the point could easily be regulated so as to prohibit a player from charging another unless he is actually "on the ball". There is also the terrible forward, on the other side, who can do a mean thing without (as he says, at least) knowing it. Her rushes about without much ceremony, and not unfrequently "does" for your half-back or back, in a very short time, but the hard and unnatural work is too much for him, and he succumbs just as his opponent is recovering. He charges the goalkeeper with too much confidence in an evil moment, and has the worst of it. Clubs who play a fair and honourable game sometimes get beaten by such opponents, but, as a rule, they come off victorious.

Scottish Football Association Annual, 1880

David Drummond Bone was a Glasgow journalist and publisher who wrote about football and cricket for the North British Daily Mail, and was also the regular Scottish football correspondent for Bell's Life in London. Sections of this piece were reprinted in Bell's Life, and in Bone's book Scottish Football Reminiscences and Sketches, a collection of articles, pen portraits and short stories published by John Menzies in 1890. Bone was the father of six sons, including artist Sir Muirhead Bone and mariner and novelist Sir David William Bone.

*"It was not football,
it was simply brutality."*

Our League Team

A Spectator, 1892

~

IF you doubt that a League football team is a
responsibility, ask one of the members of the
"playing committee". This may be said axiomati-
cally, and nearly as much of one team as another. The "finance committee" also may have
something emphatic to say on the subject. Bad
weather and a spell of ill-luck in losing matches
make its numbers sigh. The receipts then show
an alarming diminution below the average, while
the expenses of the team, with advertising and
all the rest of it, do not diminish. There is really
no knowing if at the end of the season the balance sheet may not be something disquieting in
the matter of hundreds of pounds to the bad. As
no sensible bank will advance payment without
guarantee, it may be taken for granted that the
committee has severally and jointly pledged its
good name on this count. Its interest in the performance of the League team is therefore likely
to be even more intense than that of the loud-

voiced spectators who make the welkin[11] ring with their cheers whenever the home team gains a goal in their presence.

So much for the management. In addition, however, it ought to be said that the undiscerning local public holds it accountable for the failure of the team to win matches. You should see the letters from the public which flood out evening press when such misfortune occurs. They are monstrously rude, and often make the committee writhe. Seldom do they attack the players themselves. These exulted young men can do no wrong. If they fail to do themselves justice it is the committee which is to blame for not making a fit selection of them. It may really almost be said that if our famous left winger happens to be seen in the street the worse for beer, this also is held to be the fault of the committee, and not of the left winger himself.

To turn from the committee to the players. There are about a score of them registered on our books as professionals. On average they receive fifty shillings weekly a-piece—and spend it. They also receive an immense amount of adulation, which is in its own way almost as expensive as their other habits. You can hardly wonder that they are not monuments of prudence. Their line

---

[11] Sky or heavens (Middle English).

of life is not really very exciting. All that is required of them in exchange for their week's pay
is an hour or two of practice four or five days out
of the seven and an earnest endeavour to play
their best on Saturday afternoon. Considering
that they are in the prime of young manhood,
both exercise and the game itself ought to be
thoroughly pleasurable to them—as in effect is
the case, when they keep straight.

But those sweet simple words of good Dr.
[Isaac] Watts about Satan and "idle hands" are
only too applicable to their histories. If they are
content not to add to their football income by
exertions in other directions they have a huge
number of spare hours on their hands. Their
numerous toadies and acquaintances, as well as
the publicans, know how many of these hours are
spent. It is a profound pity—but what would you
have? The rule of the committee does not claim
to be paternal or grand-paternal. The players are
grown men. They must choose their own course
in life, like the rest of us. But, to do them justice,
they are not the beer-bibbers you might suppose.
Now and then they have an extravagant carouse
which plays the dickens with their nerves on the
football field. As a rule, however, they enjoy the
dignity and honours of their high positions
shrewdly enough. Like other men, they know
that their advance in life depends upon

themselves. They know well that Argus[12] eyes are upon them to report far and wide if they show signs of exceptional talent in the field. Such talents will, in due course, bring them tempting offers from the committees of other League teams, which they are free to entertain and accept as far as their present engagements will allow. A rise from 50s to 80s or even £5 weekly is considerable in any walk of life. It is much, indeed, for the ordinary football pro, who has not had a college education, and began his career as a mechanic. Moreover the men acknowledge that their duty to the committee as well as their duty to themselves and their preferred friends demand that they should do all possible to win matches. It is whispered that in addition to their normal income they receive 10s apiece extra for every League match won. This explains the remarkably vigorous and even rough way in which they struggle for the winning goal when eighty minutes of the ninety for the game have gone and the issue is still indeterminate.

One or two of them are sure to be in the doctor's hands at time during the football season. Their pluck, however, is proverbial, and if they can hobble along they stay on the field during the match, sometimes in defiance even of the

---

[12] All-seeing giant with 100 eyes (Greek mythology).

physician's orders. About once in the season a leg or an arm gets broken, or a knee gets so twisted that the player is put *hors de combat*[13] perhaps for ever. This is a cruel blow for the invalid. Still the public is mindful of the injury, and when the benefit match occurs attends in numbers that produce a £50 note or even £100 note to be handed to the sick man as solation. It is the most useful men of the team who seem to get injured most. That, presumably, is because they are light as well as speedy. They cannot stand a heavy charge, and a foul back has an excellent chance of crippling them. But modern football legislation is taking them more and more under its protective wing, and the penalties of such foul play were never more sternly exacted than at present. On the other hand, we have five or six men in the team who are hard as nails, and go through the season as if they possessed charmed lives.

It is expected of the team to win every home match. This may be affirmed absolutely. Why should they not, it is asked. They are on their own turf, they have the moral support of their own townsfolk cheering them on, and sometimes vilifying the visitors in quite an ungentlemanly manner, and they are under the eyes of the committee, which will not be slow to mark the

---

[13] Out of the fight (French).

sins of omission on the part of any one of them. When the game is over and won, they pass through their midst of friends, who clap them on the back and shoulders, no matter how dirty they may be, and even embrace them if they have done particularly well. This incense is sweet to their nostrils, and bitter indeed is the absence of it, and the muttered innuendoes which greet them when they have failed. Nor shall they then pass a pleasant evening afterwards, telling over their battle again in an enjoyable retrospect under the glad eyes of their admirers, and with frequent glances into the flagons of beer with which they are indulged. On alien fields, however, it is another matter. Here they may receive no warmer welcome than abuse, and bits of potsherd;[14] nor shall any voice cry hurrah! when they get a goal, nor any hats fly higher in joyous celebration of their success. But if they win their fame is immediately enhanced. After a course of victories in foreign parts, the love of their followers seems to burst all reasonable bounds. The local press coins endearing nicknames and diminutives for them. The local tradesmen shower hats and boots and neckties upon them. They are photographed in their warpaint, and a large copy of the picture is hung "for all time" in the art

---

[14] Fragments of broken pottery (Middle English).

gallery, whilst smaller copies are bought by the score and hung in kitchens and parlours, as a Russian fixes his "icon" in the corner as a domestic shrine. There is, in short, no end to the testimonies of regard bestowed upon them, and a beatific vision of premier League honours comes to players and town alike, with, as a crowning triumph, the scene at the Oval, when the much-loved team proves its super-excellence by winning the English Cup into the bargain.

The Globe and syndicated, December 1892

A Meeting of Captains

Formation of the Football Association, 1863

~

ON Monday evening, Oct. 26, a meeting of
captains and other representatives of several of
the metropolitan and suburban football clubs
was held at the Freemason's Tavern, Great
Queen-street, Lincoln's Inn-fields, for the
purpose of forming an association with the object
of establishing a definite code of rules for the
regulation of the game of football. The meeting
was numerous and influential, lacking, however,
it will be observed, the presence of "The Schools",
with the exception of the Charterhouse. That
school was represented by My B. F. Hartshorne,
captain, and the other clubs and their officers
present were: Perceval House, Blackheath, Mr.
G. Shillingford, secretary; Kensington School,
Mr. W. Mackintosh, captain; Crystal Palace, Mr.
F. Day, secretary; Barnes, Mr. E. C. Morley,
captain, and Mr. P. D. Gregory, secretary;
Blackheath, Mr. F. H. Moore, captain, and Mr. F.
W. Campbell, secretary; Blackheath Proprietary
School, Mr. W. H. Gordon, captain; the

Crusaders (old public schools men); Forest, Leytonstone, Mr. J. F. Alcock, captain, and Mr. A. W. Mackenzie, secretary; N. N., Kilburn, Mr. A. Pember, captain; W. O. War Office, Mr. G. T. Wawn; and Charterhouse School, Mr. B. F. Hartshorne, captain. There were several other gentlemen present interested in the subject, who, although players, did not definitively represent any club.

Mr. PEMBER (N. N., Kilburn) was requested to take the chair, and in doing so said that it had been felt to be desirable to form some set of rules which the metropolitan clubs should adopt among themselves, as there were so many differ-ent ways of playing, in order that, when they met in friendly rivalry on other grounds the existing exceeding difficulty of "getting a goal" would be more easily overcome. It had been proposed to form an association, which should meet once a year and correct anything that was wrong if it should be necessary to do so.

Mr. E. C. MORLEY (Barnes) had hoped to have seen some of the schools represented, but their absence was attributable in all probability to the want of publicity of the fact that the meet-ing would take place. They were, however, suffi-ciently strong as football players to carry out the objects in view. He, therefore, proposed "That it advisable that a football association should be formed for the purpose of settling a code of rules for the regulation of the game of football."

Mr. A. W. MACKENZIE (Forest, Leytonstone) seconded the resolution, and hoped that the gentlemen present would form themselves into a committee to affect the purpose of the association.

Mr. B. F. HARTSHORNE (Charterhouse) could not consent at present to put his name down as a member of the association, as he thought it desirable that the public schools should be adequately represented, and take a prominent part in the movement. It was certainly most desirable that some definite set of rules for football should be generally adopted, yet, as a representative of the Charterhouse School, the only public school represented, he could not pledge himself to any course of action until he saw more clearly what the other schools did in the matter. Speaking on behalf of the Charterhouse School, he would be willing to coalesce if the other public schools would do the same, and probably at a more advanced stage of the association the opinion of the generality of the other great schools would be obtained. It certainly would be advisable, if possible, to obtain the cooperation of Rugby, Harrow, Winchester, Eton, Marlborough, Cheltenham, and other public schools.

The CHAIRMAN thought their silence probably arose from no one in particular liking to take the initiative, and put himself prominently forward. The object of the meeting was to form an association to adopt and carry out a set of rules, in doing which of course the aid of the opinion and counsel of the public schools would materially benefit them.

The resolution was then put and carried.

Mr. MACKENZIE observed that the association having been formed, it became necessary to appoint officers, and thereupon the following gentlemen were nominated and appointed:— Mr. A. Pember, president; Mr. E. C. Morley, hon sec; Mr. F. M. Campbell (Blackheath), treasurer.

It was then agreed that the subscription should be £1 1s per annum, and that the annual general meeting should take place in the month of September on a day to be named. All clubs of one year's standing to be eligible to join the association, and to send two members as representatives.

The majority of the gentlemen present put down their names to form the committee, but Mr. Hartshorne declined to do so for the reasons he had assigned. The hon secretary was then requested to communicate with the captains and secretaries of the different public schools, to ask them if they would co-operate with the association, and also to give publicity to the time of the next meeting by advertisement in the sporting journals. A cordial vote of thanks to the chairman brought the proceedings to an end.

Bell's Life in London, 31 October 1863

Of the thirteen clubs represented at this first meeting of the Football Association, eleven became founding members. Among the notable attendees, Arthur Pember and particularly Edward Cobb Morley can be regarded among the principal founders of association football. John Alcock was the brother of Charlie Alcock. Mr. Wawn of the War Office represented the Civil Service football club. Among the "other gentlemen present" were representatives of Bucks FC and Surbiton FC. Barnes, Blackheath, Blackheath Proprietary School, Civil Service, Crusaders, Crystal Palace, Kensington School, Forest, N. N., Perceval House and Surbiton joined, while Bucks and Charterhouse declined. The Crystal Palace club is no relation to the modern club of the same name. Forest changed its name to Wanderers in 1864. N. N. is the "No Name" club of Kilburn. In subsequent weeks, following disagreement over the laws of the game, several founding members (led by Blackheath) left the Association before a game had been played.

The First Match

President's Side v Secretary's Side, 1864

~

THE first match played actually under the new rules of the Football Association took place on Saturday, Jan 9, in Battersea Park, amongst the members of the various clubs now forming the association.

The sides were chosen by the Messrs Alcock (both capital players); and as president and the secretary "on this occasion only and for their joint benefit" took opposite sides, we class them thus:—

The President's side: Messrs A. Pember, C. W. Alcock, H. W. Chambers, A. M. Tebbutt, Gray, Drew, Graham, Cutbill, Morton, J. Turner, Morris, Renshaw, Leuchars, and Scott.

The Secretary's side: Messrs E. C. Morley, J. F. Alcock, C. M. Tebbutt, Lloyd, C. Hewett, G. T. Wawn, J. P. Phillips, Innes, McCalmont, Needham, H. Baker, A. Baker, Hughes, and Jackson.

Where all played well, individual mention hardly comes within reportable scope; but

Messrs Pember, Hewett, Morley, Chambers, and both the Alcocks especially distinguished themselves. Mr. Chambers, the able representative of the Sheffield Football Club, gave a capital taste of his quality. The president's side, after some spirited play, obtained two goals, the final kick in each instance being obtained by Mr. C. W. Alcock.

In the evening the members of the association dined together at the Grosvenor Hotel, Pimlico, under the presidency of Mr. A. Pember. "Success to Football, irrespective of class or creed," was heartily drunk, and a most agreeable evening passed.

Bell's Life in London, 16 January 1864

This first association football match was played between two teams of 14 players. It was not uncommon for association games to be played with more than 11 players on each side into the 1870s. The scorer of the first two goals in association football was, almost inevitably, Charlie Alcock. Other notable players include John Alcock, FA president Arthur Pember, secretary Edward Cobb Morley, future England goalkeeper Alec Morton, and Harry Waters Chambers of Sheffield FC.

An Action for Libel

Newton Heath v the Birmingham Gazette, 1894

~

AN ACTION for libel was brought recently at the
Manchester Assizes, before Mr. Justice Day and
a special jury, by the Newton Heath Football
Club against the Birmingham Gazette. Mr. Shee,
Q.C., and Mr. Bradbury appeared for the
plaintiffs; Mr. Gully, Q.C., M.P., and Mr. C. A.
Russell for the defendants. The libel complained
of was that the plaintiffs had been playing a
match at Newton Heath with the West
Bromwich Albion team. The club was a member
of the Football Association, the Football League,
and the Football Combination. Being a member
of these associations was of considerable
importance in this case. The League consisted of
sixteen of the best clubs in the country. The
plaintiff club was a company that engaged
professionals as well as amateur players, and it
had become so noted that it was in the first
division of the Football League. That fact tended
to draw spectators, and increase the receipts at

the "gate". It was therefore of considerable importance that the players should not be accused of improper play. Mr. Shee read the full text of the criticism in the Gazette, which appeared on the 16th October, two days after the match.

In referring to the match, the Gazette said:— "It was not football, it was simply brutality, and if these are to be the tactics Newton Heath are compelled to adopt to win their matches the sooner the Football Association deal severely with them the better it will be for the game generally. At the very commencement the Newton Heath forwards went like tigers, and through a misskick by [Mark] Nicholson they literally swept all before them, and scored the first goal. This was immediately followed by a second, scored in a similar way, but one of the Newton Heath forwards was mean enough to kick [goalkeeper Joe] Reader on the ankle even after the ball was in the net. The Albion after this had much of the best of the game, suffering hard lines in front of goal, [Tom] Pearson once hitting the crossbar with a terrific shot. It looked any odds on the Albion winning the first ten minutes in the second half, when [George] Perrins kicked [Alf] Geddes in the spine of the back, raising a lump as big as a duck-egg, when he unfortunately had to retire. Charlie Perry was also limping about, and the only man who appeared able to play the Newton Heath men back in their own coin was Nicholson. It was astonishing what cowards they appeared when tackled firmly, but they managed to rush a couple more goals, although the Albion had quite as much of the play as their opponents. It was simply weight and brute force that enabled Newton Heath to win, but in spite of everything the Albion looked like defeating them until Geddes had to leave the field. [John] Peden at last was guilty of some dirty tricks. Reader had no chance whatsoever with either of the goals scored against him, as they were all obtained from within a couple of yards of him, and were the results of rushes and wild kicking. Although it was a mistake by Nicholson to let Newton Heath in at first, he played a great game afterwards, while Horton did well also until he received a kick at the back of the head. I notice that next week Newton Heath have to play Burnley, and if they both play in their ordinary style it will perhaps create an extra run of business for the undertakers."

Mr. Shee said that if foul play took place at a match the Football Association was ready to take notice of it. The association wanted no incitement to do so from the Birmingham Gazette; the association knew its own business better than anybody else. The Gazette had said that the match was stopped, but it was not stopped.

Mr. Gully said there was no libel against the company which employed the football players.

The Judge said he could not see what the club was going to do with it. It was not an action to recover damages, as if the company dealt in commercial transactions.

Mr. Bradbury said it was disparaging the company.

The Judge: But do you put it on a commercial basis?

Mr. Gully: Do you say it is a gate money action?

Mr. Bradbury: We do not say that it is a company to make profits, but we have to pay expenses and pay our officers and players, and if we were to be struck out of the Football Association and the League we should suffer because our matches would not be so important. We could not play in certain matches at all, and so many people would not come to see out play.

The Judge said he could not see any charges against the club. It was a charge against some persons who played in the team. The club could not be responsible for what the team might do.

Ultimately his lordship ruled that there was no attack upon the football club as a company.

A large number of witnesses were called in support of the plaintiffs' case.

Alfred H. Albut, secretary of the [Newton Heath] club, stated that he saw the match, and thought it a fair ordinary league match. There was nothing in the conduct of the Newton Heath team to call for reprobation. The teams were fairly evenly matched.

Cross-examined by Mr. Gully, Mr. Albut said that three of the players for Newton Heath in a match at Derby were severely criticised by the Derby papers. These were suspended, two for a fortnight. The referee was suspended for a year. (Laughter.) The alleged roughness was of such a character that if it had taken place the referee should have ordered every man off the field. He could not remember whether at a recent football dinner he had said "the Newton Heath men are guilty of rough conduct, but they have such a clever way of doing it that the referee cannot find them out." (Laughter.) It was a very merry dinner. (Laughter.)

The Judge: Were you too drunk to be able to remember?

Mr. Albut: I can't say. I can't remember. (Laughter.)

J. H. Strawson, the referee of the match out of which the alleged libel arose, said the account on the Birmingham Gazette was a very false account. Reader of Newton Heath complained to him of being kicked, but he told Reader that he had watched the game closely, and that he had not seen him kicked. He did not see Geddes or any other player kicked in the back. He considered the match was fair and sportsmanlike. No complaint was made during the game. In reply to Mr. Gully, the witness said he had made the remark that the West Bromwich Albion did not appeal enough for breach of rules. He gave several free kicks to the Albion men. The crowd was well behaved and orderly.

E. A. Davies, sub-editor of the Manchester Evening News, said he was present at the match, and thought it one of the best contested and fairest games that he had seen under Association Rules. The description of the game as "mere brutality" was, in his opinion, absurd.

The Rev. B. Reid, rector of St. Luke's, Miles Platting, said he had a long football experience. He saw the match in question and was rather disappointed with it. He thought it was an unusually tame game.

Henry P. Renshaw, Thomas Horgan, and Thomas Axon, newspaper reporters, described the game as being very fairly played. Mr. Gully, for the defence, said this was the first time he had ever heard of a company formed for the purpose of playing a popular game coming forward as a trading company and claiming damages for the interference with business caused by

the appearance of an adverse report. They came
forward as a trading concern, and claimed damages because of the paragraph in which it was
said that if Newton Heath and Burnley played in
their ordinary style they would encourage the
undertaker. This seemed to him to be the very
madness of litigation. How on earth was this
company defamed or one penny the worse for a
statement of this kind? Was it the case, then,
that people would be frightened away from the
matches of the Newton Heath Club by the advertisement that there was the chance of seeing a
leg broken? (Laughter.) To announce any event—
such as a man dropping from a balloon, wheeling
a man across a rope 100ft. from the ground, or
dropping from a great height into a pool of water
6ft. deep—was sure to attract a large crowd.
Therefore if the defendants announced that there
was likely to be work for the undertakers it
would attract more spectators than ever, and the
receipts at the gate would be enlarged. The article in the Gazette was written in perfect good
faith. The writer of the article, it must be remembered, was invited to come and witness the
game and to express his own views on it. Those
views might not commend themselves to everybody, but if honestly expressed they did not give
cause for action. If the writer saw, or even honestly thought he saw, a kick which was a foul,

and reported that kick, then, even though he might be mistaken, he was not liable to action. The referee was not altogether an impartial witness. He probably did not want to be carried off the pitch on a shutter—(laughter)—and therefore his tendency was not in the direction of turning two or three of the home players off their field in the presence of a crowd of 10,000 enthusiasts. It was notorious that the game having been thrown altogether into the hands of professionals had become vulgarised and brutalised, and that the temper of crowds who witnessed it was rather un-English. All the more need was there for a perfectly free criticism of the game.

William Jephcott, the writer of the article in the Birmingham Gazette, described the game in detail, and generally bore out the statements made in the article. Reader, he said, was intentionally and unfairly kicked. Peden several times put his foot out, a very dangerous practice. Mr. Jephcott said his account was fair and honest, and he had a better chance of seeing the game than other reporters, as he only took shorthand notes.

John Horton, a member of the Albion team, said he had played left back in the Newton Heath match. The play of Newton Heath was very rough. It was rougher than usual. Peden was guilty of particularly rough conduct towards him, and caused him great pain. Witness did not appeal to the referee. He thought the referee did not see the stroke. He played in the match of the following week.

Geddes, who played outside left forward in the West Bromwich team, Nicholson, Burns, and other players agreed that the Newton Heath men were very rough in their play.

The Judge said the question was whether the report was a fair report of what took place.

Mr. Shee pointed out that the defendants had not called a single independent witness to support their cases. All their witnesses were interested persons, while his witnesses included the men not only who denied the acts against them, but pressmen, a clergyman, and other persons who had no interest in either side. It was singular that not a single comment had been made in the press-box that afternoon of foul or rough play. The evidence was overwhelming that the match had been a thoroughly well-contested game, played on the best of terms, and free from brute force and illegality.

The jury found a verdict for the plaintiffs.

The Judge said that having regard to the general character of the action and the result of it, the jury evidently considered—and he agreed with them—that it was a case which ought not to have been brought, and the plaintiffs ought not to obtain further fruits of their success than had been awarded by the jury; therefore, each party paying their own costs would carry out the views of the jury, and most properly so.

Judgement was then entered for the plaintiffs for one farthing, but no costs.

Manchester Times, 2 & 5 March 1894 and *Sydney Mail*, 14 & 21 April 1894

Newton Heath won the match concerned, at Bank Street on 14 October 1893, by four goals to one. The libel judgement had far-reaching consequences. "The Birmingham Gazette has rendered service to the football world, and to newspaper reporters, by its defence of the action raised by the Newton Heath Football Club," commented the Dart (9 March 1894). "The misfortune is that the Gazette has to pay its own costs, and one farthing of damages. But, as a result, it is improbable that any other football club will venture to imitate Newton Heath." Newton Heath changed its name to Manchester United in 1902.

How to Play at Football

George Forrest, 1862

~

OF all out-door games for winter, or, indeed, for any cold day, Football is *facile princeps*,[15] king and chief.

Only in cold, or at least in cool weather, can this game be played, as it requires such incessant movement and such strenuous exertion on the part of every player, that no-one would be able to endure a spirited game played in the summer time.

Cricket, although a far more scientific game, and also played with a ball, is practically limited to a few months in the year; for of the twenty-two players engaged in a game, little more than half are actually playing at any one time, and of that number the greater part are standing still with their hands on their knees, looking out for balls which may not come in their direction during the whole course of the game. Even the bowler would not be able to direct his missile with sufficient

---

[15] Easily first (Latin).

certainty upon the nard and ice-bound ground, the batters could hardly grasp their weapons in their half-frozen fingers, and the fieldsmen would assuredly be unable to stop a ball in hands benumbed and stiffened with cold.

So, during the winter months, the game is necessarily abandoned, the bats are returned to their baize cases, the stumps laid up in ordinary, and the balls put away until the kindly sun shall unlock the icy bands of the earth, and restore the cricketers to the enjoyment of their loved game.

Again, the expense of the two games is entirely disproportionate. We all know how costly is the management of a cricket club as an association, quite independent of the individual expense of the members, who must spend no inconsiderable sum in the various appurtenances of the game before they can be admitted to take part in a regular match, or, indeed, can be at all considered players.

But with football, the only expense consists of the purchasing of two balls, four long sticks, two short ones, and a bladder now and then. The two balls are requisite in order that, if an accident should happen to the one in play, the reserve ball may at once be substituted, and the game continued, while the wounded ball is being repaired by a non-player. The process of mending an injured ball will be presently described.

This game has lately been brought into public notice, and its rules submitted to investigation.

At present, the rules seem to be entirely arbitrary, depending on the local regulations of the spot where the game is played. Considerable inconvenience is caused by this irregularity, as a match between two schools or two counties is almost impracticable, while the regulations are so loose and diverse, that hardly any two of the players may adhere to the same system.

Some places, led by the Rugby system, employ a set of rules remarkable for their number and complexity, employing more technical terms, and even more difficult to comprehend, than the rules of billiards. Other places have their own peculiar rules—not so many as are involved in those of Rugby, but still, in our opinion, too complicated for general use. We have read very carefully every acknowledged code of rules, and applying to them the practical experience of some years, and many a glorious game lost and won, shall give our readers the benefit of our opinion thereon.

Be it, however, premised, that we by no means consider the subject as finally settled. We shall closely watch the progress of correspondence, and keep our readers acquainted with the state of opinion.

To notice all the existing systems would

occupy the whole of the space allotted to this article, and we shall, therefore, content ourselves with putting forward a plan of the game, with a few very simple rules, assuring our readers that the system has been thoroughly tested, and found to answer well by practical experience.

The necessaries for this game are few and simple.

First, get two *good* leathern football cases, made to close with a leathern thong, and a separate tongue of thinner, but stiff and strong material. A shoemaker will generally manufacture the cases better than those which are purchased ready made, unless a ball be procured from the old established shops in London. Take care that the seams are closely drawn, and that the rotundity of ball is true.

Next, purchase from the nearest butcher a pair of the largest ox bladders, telling him the purpose for which they are wanted. When detached or taken from the animal, they are very unpromising bits of affairs, thick, short, and flabby, and apparently so unfit to dilate the lather case, that a dozen or two might be placed in each case without inconvenience. Undeterred, however, by the unsightly task, put the bladders into water, warm if possible, and let them soak while you get a rather thin quill and some strong twine.

After soaking has been continued for a few hours, cut off the feather, and just a little of the tip of the quill, so as to form a tube, narrow at the point; insert it into the neck of the bladder, and by gently manoeuvring with the fingers, get it at least an inch through the aperture, and tie it firmly, so as to hold it tightly in its place. Make a loose knot in the twine, pass it over the quill, so as to bring it just below the point (see fig. 1), and, holding the two ends of the string in the hands, take the large end of the quill in the mouth, and blow into the bladder until it is as full as it can be made. Pull the string tight, so as to prevent the air escaping, and the first step is made. Now take it to some very smooth board or table; lay it on its side; put the palms of both hands on it; lean rather heavily, but not so as to burst the membrane, and roll it backwards and forwards like a cook with a rolling-pin in making a pie. Presently the walls of the bladder become thinner, and the whole substance greatly enlarges, so that, instead of being tight and roundish, it is quite loose and flabby.

Then untie the lower string, inflate the bladder afresh, and you will be surprised to find how it has enlarged by this simple process, which must be continually repeated until the bladder, when properly expanded, is at least half as large again as the case into which it has to be forced.

FIG. 1.

FIG. 2.

The next business is to inflate the ball—a task requiring some strength and much care.

Let the case, but not the tongue, lie in water for a short time, so as to make it tolerably pliable; untie the lower string of the bladder, squeeze out all the air, and, but patting and grasping, reduce it to a nearly cylindrical shape. Slip the lower end into the case, and blow as much air into it as the lungs can drive, tying it very firmly with the lower string. It will then puff out like a great hour glass and look like the left-hand figure in the accompanying illustration (fig. 2). Unite the upper string, remove the quill, and put it away for further use.

The next process is to grasp the upper part of the bladder firmly with the hands, getting some one to assist by holding the case, and begin to twist from the top downwards until you have worked the top into a screw, and so forced all the air into the ball. No process is half so efficacious as this, or gives so good a rebounding power to the ball. Twenty pairs of blacksmith's bellows could not equal the work of two boys and one pair of lungs, if rightly managed.

Now get a couple of strong leather boot-laces—those of the white horse-leather are the best, and least breakable; pass one through the two centre holes of the gaping aperture; tuck the screw under the leather case by dint of mixed strength and adroitness; slip the tongue over it, and hold it down while your assistant ties the lace as firmly as he can manage, so as to keep the tongue down and the sides partly together. (See central figure in the illustration, fig. 2.) If this precaution is neglected, the tongue is always slipping out at one end as fast as the lace is tightened at the other, and thus wastes time and patience sadly.

The next process is to lace the thongs so firmly that the tops of the opening are brought fairly together. The ends are then woven among the crossed thongs, and the ball is complete, bounding in a very perfect fashion, and quite elastic.

Some of our readers may object that the indiarubber balls sold in the shops are already inflated, and save all the trouble and mess incidental to blowing up a ball of this kind. To this remark we answer that indiarubber balls are but delusions. They are very pretty to look at, but are sadly liable to burst, while the least wound from a thorn or splinter ruins them at once, for they cannot be mended except by the makers. Whereas, one of our bladder-balls is little the worse for wear for a wound, and can be perfectly repaired even in the field. We therefore admonish our readers to take the word of experienced advisers, and not to buy an indiarubber ball for out-door play, as they value their time, their pocket, and their patience.

Of course it will be understood that two balls are to be prepared simultaneously. Having the balls, the next matter is to make the "goals" through which the ball is to pass. These are very simple, and may be set up in two minutes. Get four long sticks or slender poles, about eight feet long, forked at the top like those employed by laundresses to keep their lines off the ground, and two straight sticks without forks. These are arranged as shown in fig. 3. If you want to be very neat, or you cannot procure forked poles, get a carpenter to cut rough poles of elm, and have an iron fork driven at the tops. Common washing poles are just suited for this, and if the butt-ends are shod with sharp iron points, nothing more can be desired.

These are all the needful implements, and we

will now prepare for action by shouldering our poles and starting off for the field. It is not a bad precaution to put on the worst suit of clothes, as few energetic players get through a game without tumbling down, and never without much earthy sign of their labour. The field should be large, and, if possible, free from thorns, which make sad havoc with the balls, often disabling the second before the first can be repaired.

The ground is laid out with the two goals pitched exactly opposite each other, at any distance agreed upon, or as may be suitable to the ground. This operation should be conducted under the direction of the two captains of the sides who are to play. Seven feet is a good distance between the two poles. Two long lines are then traced parallel to each other, and passing through the bases of the poles. These are termed goal lines, and may be conveniently marked out with string and pegs, if the ground may not be cut up; otherwise, a slight trench is the best mark. A small hole is then cut in the very centre, or a peg of wood is driven into the ground to mark the spot.

The captains now disperse the men according to their ability, each being obliged to keep his men on his own side of the hole or peg. Each side now has to drive the ball through the opposite goal, and to guard their own from being taken.

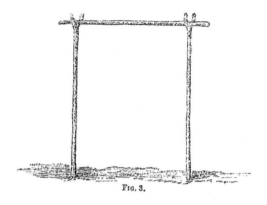

FIG. 3.

The struggle begins by having the ball thrown perpendicular from the peg, so as to fall evenly and fairly in the centre. Sometimes the mode of starting the ball is different, the two sides drawing lots for the start, the winners proceeding to a spot in front of their own goal, and being allowed a fair kick as the ball lies in the ground. In our opinion, however, the perpendicular fling of the ball is the best. We shall now lay down the few rules that are needful for playing the game:—

1. The game being essentially *Foot*-ball, no player may take up the ball from the ground.

2. If a player can catch the ball in the air, he may take a hand-kick without the other side being permitted to interfere. (A hand-kick consists in dropping the ball from the hands and kicking it on its fall.)

3. If such a player shall drop the ball acciden-

tally, or in any way touch the ground with it, the opposite side may attack it.

4. If the ball passes outside or over the goal, and beyond the goal line, the junior player of the side which drove it over shall fetch the ball, stand twelve paces to the right of the centre hole or peg, and throw it gently to the centre without favour to either side. (The object of this rule will be explained presently.)

5. Any kicking, except at the ball, is prohibited.

6. The ball must be *kicked* through the goal, not struck or thrown, or touch any part of any player of the same side, except the foot of him who kicks it. In such a case, the ball is fetched back, as in Rule 4.

These few and simple remarks are, we believe, all that are really useful. This 4th rule is used because it sometimes happens that irritable players, finding the enemy's goal too well defended, wilfully kick the ball far beyond, hoping to exhaust their opponents, and thus needlessly prolong the game. It is a mark of bad play, as well as unmanliness, to drive the ball where it can be of no use, and the penalty deprives the offending side of the junior player while he throws in the ball so as to deter them from repeating their error.

In one large school, a number of wretched little junior boys were stationed in lines from each goal, to stop the ball from going out of its course, and had to stand shivering in the cold while their superiors were playing, being sure of punishment if they allowed the ball to pass them. This system, however, technically called "kicking-in", is now, we believe, being disused.

In disposing the men, the best way is to place a good player in front of goal, so as to stop the ball from being kicked between the poles over the heads of the players, as might otherwise be achieved by a hand-kick, and as, indeed, is the object of that privilege. Another moderately good player is stationed about half way between the goal and the centre peg, and those two are said technically to "play back", the others "playing up". The goal-keeper never leaves his post except at the utmost emergency, such as the ball being driven towards the goal by several opponents, and no one but himself to prevent the game from being lost. He then would dash at the ball, hoping to get it out of the line, and so to give time for his own party to come to the rescue.

We venture to think readers of this magazine will find that these rules are amply sufficient for the playing of the game of Football with spirit, and at the same time for guarding against the various contingencies which arise in the severe struggles incident to the game. We prefer the style of goal mentioned, because there can be no doubt whether a ball has passed through or not; it is just high and wide enough to give many chances to the opponents and at the same time is not too large to be guarded by a single player.

In the Rugby game, the two side poles are eighteen feet high, the cross-bar is ten feet from the ground, and ball has to pass over the bar and between the posts. This is so difficult a feat to achieve, even when there is no one to arrest the ball, that a game is often played for several days without a single goal being gained. The game is, in consequence, most needlessly prolonged, and the best play may be frustrated by a gust of wind or other accident occurring just at the time of kicking at the goal.

After each goal, the players usually change goals, so as to make everything perfectly fair on both sides, and neutralize the effect of sloping ground, favouring winds, &c., which might otherwise preponderate in favour of one side.

We promised our readers to show them how to mend a ball if pricked buy a thorn, or otherwise injured.

Unbind the thongs, loosen the neck of the bladder, and squeeze out all the air under it, remove from the case, and then reinflate it, holding it to the cheek , and squeezing it to find out the aperture. This found, put a pin or splinter of wood through it to mark the precise spot,

Fig. 4.

and push a little round pebble down the neck of the bladder. The shot called No. 1 or No. 2, is, however, better than pebbles, and it is as well to have half a dozen shot always ready.

Then hold the bladder with the injured part downwards, so as to get the shot exactly over the wound, withdraw the pin, and seize the shot with the fingers, pinching the membrane firmly round it, and keeping the hole upon the shot so that the lead is visible. Get some one to loop a piece of very thin, but strong twine or silk, just above the shot, as in the right-hand figure in fig. 4, and then tie it firmly as in the left-hand figure. The bladder will now be perfectly mended and good as ever. The reader will see that the use of the shot is sufficient to prevent the thread from working off in the course of play. Should the hole be a very large one, a pebble must be employed. The bladder will bear six or seven such repairs before it is rendered useless.

Before returning the bladder to the case, the leather should be turned inside out, and carefully examined, not only to the eye, but by the hand, in order to discover any little thorn or splinter that may be projecting through the leather and be likely to cause further injury.

Every Boy's Magazine, February 1862

George Forrest, a former schoolmaster, wrote widely on various sports under his own name and under nom de plumes. This article appeared in the first issue of Every Boy's Magazine, published by George Routledge and edited by his son Edmund, more than 18 months before the newly-formed Football Association drew up the first official laws of the game.

"All's fair in love and war – and in modern Association football."

How Referees Are Tricked

A Referee, 1892

~

ALL'S fair in love and war—and in modern Association football. I once refereed in a match between two well known teams which, to separate them from professional combustions, dub themselves "gentlemanly". Bogus claims were made by one side until I became wearied, so I said to one of the players during a lull in the game— "You know very well that that last shot was not a goal".

"Of course I do," he replied, "but I didn't know that you did, and nothing is lost by appealing."

That is exactly the standing motto of the average professional footballer—"Nothing is lost by appealing." When the goal is hotly attacked it is a regular dodge for the keeper or one of the backs to shout "Offside!" and many a time have I seen a free kick result and the goal thereby cleared. Another trick that often pays is practised during a "bully" or a crush in goal. One of the defending side will deliberately handle the ball, and then claim a foul for hands—a claim which is allowed sadly too often. Or, if a goal is scored, some custodians will occasionally bring back the ball with all the coolness imaginable, and declare that the attackers claimed and must take a free kick. More than once to my knowledge this dodge has meant all the difference between the winning and losing of a match. Touching this matter of "hands", and of the difficulty which a referee sometimes has in deciding between conflicting claims, I remember a very funny experience. From a corner kick the ball was dropped right in front of goal, and was shot through. At the same moment a "smack" was heard, and immediately the cry of "Hands!" was raised. The referee was inclined to allow the claim, but the centre forward of the side which had scored drew attention to his ear, which was red and evidently painful. The centre, it seemed, went to head the ball just as the goal-keeper tried to fist out, and so received a blow on the ear that nearly stunned him. Some quick passing and a cross-shot into goal frequently result in the ball going just inside the posts. The referee is unable to keep up with the ball, and consequently is uncertain whether it went between the posts or not. "Smart" goal-keepers, in these circumstances, quickly pick up the ball, and kick off from goal, as if it had gone outside. The attacking team appeal, as a matter of course, for the goal; but the referee, not being certain, gives the defenders, as magistrates give prisoners, "the benefit of the doubt". I remember an instance of this kind of thing which occurred in a cup tie. One of the full-backs deliberately stepped forward in order to obstruct the view of the referee, and a legitimate goal was disallowed. On the other hand, I have heard it said, though I have never seen it myself, that weak-willed referees have been deceived by confident appeals when the ball has gone outside the post. All this, however, is done away with by using the nets, which have recently been adopted. About foul play—tripping and "settling" players—no referee can say all he thinks. Enough that a good deal of what is ascribed to accident is really malicious injury. The referees are deceived, and so is nearly everybody else.

Cassell's Saturday Journal and syndicated, December 1892

International Association Match

England v Scotland, 1872

~

THIS important match was played on the West
of Scotland Cricket Ground, on Saturday, and
resulted in a drawn game, after a splendid display of football in the really scientific sense of
the word, and a most determined effort on the
part of the representatives of the two nationali-
ties to overcome each other. The only thing
which saved the Scotch from defeat, considering
the powerful forward play of England, was the
magnificent defensive play and tactics shown by
their backs, which was also taken advantage of
by the forwards. When the players came to the
scratch it was at once seen that the English had
greatly the advantage in weight and appearance
(averaging about 12st against 10st of their opponents), and the odds were freely offered in favour
of "John Bull", who had a really typical represen-
tation in the team. The Scotch players, on the
other hand, although slightly built, were exceedingly wiry and tough, and, belonging (at least the
bulk of them) to one club, were at home in each

other's society, and knew what was required of them. It was naturally thought that the English players, although showing fine individual play, would be deficient in working together, belonging as they did to so many different clubs, but the game had not proceeded far when this allusion was dispelled like mist at the approach of the sun, for the magnificent dribbling of the English captain [Cuthbert Ottaway], [Arnold] Kirke-Smith, and [John] Brockbank, seconded as it was by the fine back play of [Reginald Courtenay] Welch, [Ernest] Greenhalgh, and [Frederick] Chappel, was greatly admired by the immense concourse of spectators, who kept the utmost order, and although now and again showing some partiality to their own champions (possibly on account of it being the anniversary of Scotland's patron saint), a fine piece of play on the English side did not pass uncheered.

The Scotch had choice of the ground, and elected the pavilion end, from which they had the benefit of a slight decline, which terminated at the English goal. The game had not long commenced, when the English forwards, led by the stalwart form of their captain, began to show themselves conspicuous, the former making a splendid run till within a short distance of the Scotch goal, where one or two long shies were made without effect. In a short time thereafter

SKETCHES AT THE INTERNATIONAL
FOOTBALL MATCH BY WILLIAM RALSTON,
THE GRAPHIC, DECEMBER 1872

the Scotch forwards securing the ball which had been so well been put out of the way by their backs, sent it flying forward to neutral territory, where it was kept for some time, until [Jerry] Weir, [Alexander] Rhind, and [David] Wotherspoon, assisted by [Robert] Leckie, brought it safely through the enemy's backs, and forward to the goal line, where it was knocked about for some time, till a fine effort on the part of Welch, and a splendid run on the part of Ottaway, who received quite an ovation for his magnificent dribbling, had the ball up to the Scotch quarters in a twinkling, passing on his way quite a shoal of opposing feet. The success which attended his efforts, however, was brief, for after a short scrummage for possession the ball was nicely piloted by Ker and Weir, the latter of whom displayed great skill in its management. After this a most determined rush was made for the English goal, and the united exertions of [Robert] Smith, Weir, and Wotherspoon, were nearly crowned with success, for Leckie, who got the ball well in line, made an effort to kick goal, and had the ball only gone an inch under instead of landing on the tape, Scotland would have been the victor. This was the signal for a loud burst of enthusiasm on the part of the spectators, who thought a goal had been secured by one of their champions. After the appeal had been settled half time was called, and the English having the advantage possessed by their opponents during the first half of the game soon drove the Scotch before them and put them on the defensive. The tactics, however, of the Scotch team, in which they clearly outwitted the enemy, never shone to greater advantage than when brought to bay, and it was not long till a successful manoeuvre on the part of Ker and [William "Billy" Muir] MacKinnon, and wrought out by [Robert] Gardner, who had taken R. Smith's place (the former keeping goal, which he defended admirably), the leather was safely deposited in neutral territory; but the watchful eyes of the brave English forwards only allowed it to remain there for an instant, and off it went back to the Scotch goal, where it remained for a long time. All the tactics possessed by the English team were here put into account, the ball ever and anon going backwards and forwards in front of the Scotch goal, until one of the backs made a strenuous effort to get the ball home, but the goal-keeper saved the stronghold against all attempts. With only five minutes to play, a most determined effort on behalf of the Scotch to free their goal from danger was successful, and Ker, who played throughout in a masterly style, made a fine run up to the English line just a time was called, the match thus ending in a draw.

When such brilliant play was shown by both sides it would almost be superfluous to "individualise", but it must be admitted that the dribbling of the English forwards, especially Ottaway and Kirke-Smith, was greatly admired by all, and the splendid all-round play of Ker and Weir for Scotland deserve more than a passing notice. Shortly after the match, and before the players left the field, three cheers were given for the English champions, and also the Scotch. Mr. [Charlie] Alcock, who has not yet recovered from the accident, which he sustained a fortnight ago, acted as umpire for England, while Mr. [H. N.] Smith, president of the Queen's Park Club, acted in that capacity for Scotland. The return match will take place, we believe, in February in London. The English team were entertained to dinner in the Royal Hotel, where toasts suitable to the occasion were proposed and responded to.

Sides:

ENGLAND.—C. J. Ottaway (Oxford University) (captain), C. J. Chenery (Crystal Palace), J. C. Clegg (Sheffield), E. H. Greenhalgh (Notts), F. M. Chappell (Oxford University), C. J. Morice (Barnes Club), R. C. Welch (Wanderers), W. J. Maynard (1st Surrey Rifles), R. Barker (Hertfordshire Rangers), A. Kirke-Smith (Oxford University), and J. Brockbank (Cambridge University).

SCOTLAND.—R. W. Gardner (captain), J. J. Thomson and W. Ker (Granville) (backs), J. Weir, J. Taylor, R. Leckie, W. McKinnon, A Rhind, D. Wotherspoon (Queen's Park), and J. Smith and R. Smith (South Norwood).

Bell's Life in London, 7 December 1872

This first "official" international football match (following five "unofficial" representative matches) was played on 30 November 1872 at the West of Scotland Cricket Club ground at Hamilton Crescent in Partick. There were around 4,000 spectators, and entry cost a shilling. Although he was the principal organiser, Charlie Alcock was prevented from playing in the match by injury. Robert Gardner and Robert Smith shared goalkeeping duties for Scotland, and Robert Barker and William Maynard did likewise for England. The referee is named in several sources as William Keay, of Queen's Park.

The sketch artist William Ralston (1848-1911), from Glasgow, was a regular contributor to the Graphic, a weekly illustrated newspaper published by William Luson Thomas.

Association Football and How to Master It

Mr. G. O. Smith Talks about the Great Game
C. Duncan Lewis, 1896

~

NOW that the Football season has commenced, the readers of Chums will naturally be expecting some hints on the winter pastime—hints as to how they may save their goal and their shins at the same time. No authority is better qualified to give advice on this subject than Mr. G. O. Smith, the famous International Association footballer. Mr. Smith is an ideal athlete. A brilliant footballer, a fine cricketer, the old Oxonian is equally at home when he is playing a winning game or working like a Trojan to save his side from defeat.

I don't suppose it is necessary to remind readers that it was Mr. Smith who practically won the last University cricket match for Oxford. His great score of a hundred and more was compiled at a critical moment, and when the Dark Blues were badly in need of runs; but if he made one of the biggest scores that has ever been recorded in

MR. G. O. SMITH

a University match it was only what was to be expected from the popular old Charterhouse boy. If everyone else in the team fails and pulls a face as long as the Monument, Mr. G. O. Smith can always be depended upon to shatter the rising hopes of the opposing side. It is very cruel, no doubt, but he can't help it; it is in his nature to!

When I wrote to Mr. Smith the other day and told him that the readers of Chums were anxious to make his acquaintance, he very kindly offered to answer any questions I might put to him.

At many schools I could name, the boy who doesn't take his place in the football field is quietly—well, licked. The licking is usually severe enough to ensure his presence between the goal-posts at regular intervals for the remainder of the term.

I asked Mr. Smith his opinion of compulsory football—whether he thinks a boy ought to be made to learn football for his health's sake, just as he has to fill his head with algebraical solutions for his brain's sake.

"In compulsory games, as a whole, I do not believe," he replied. "They may be and often are useful for very young boys who would not play unless they were made to, and who must often look back thankfully to the compulsion that has been exercised; but for older boys, who have arrived at an age to see that playing games is better than loafing, I do not think they are at all necessary; football is played by them because it is football, and a game directly it becomes an imposed task loses half its charms.

"Football, in my opinion, is best enjoyed and best played at schools where it is not nominally compulsory, but where public opinion practically makes everyone keen to play. In such a case football loses all sense of a task which must be undergone, and becomes a game at which it is the desire of all to excel."

"Do you consider it a very healthy game?"

"I don't think there can be a doubt that football is good for the health. For a strong boy an hour and a half's exercise or violent exercise is not at all a bad thing, and I can remember playing three hours on end and never feeling the worse, though I fancy that was rather too much. Of course, where a weak boy is concerned it may be overdone, but in an ordinary case the exercise to be obtained at football cannot, I think, be considered detrimental to health."

"But what about the boy, Mr. Smith, who would be much better for a sound, healthy game, but who wraps himself up in shawls and mustard plaisters[16] and takes snuff to assist him in shamming a cold, then gets the doctor to certify

---

[16] A remedy for respiratory complaints.

that he is unfit to play? Does this kind of youth as a rule grow up weaker than the boy who regularly dons his jersey and goes through the game like a trump?"

"As far as my experience goes, the boy who enters keenly and heartily into the game will necessarily prove a better and stronger fellow than the one who shams to avoid it. The former will almost certainly be energetic in other things as well as football, while the latter will probably shirk his other duties as he has shirked his games."

Since most of us are eager to shine on the football field, can you give me some useful recipe for the making of a first-rate footballer?"

"It is hard to recommend any particular course to a boy who wishes to become a good football player. The saying *nascitur, non fit*[17] applies, I think, to football as well as other things: a boy must have it born in him to become really great at the game. Of course, perseverance will succeed, as a rule, in turning out a moderate player, but unless perseverance is aided by an innate skill it will not produce a first-class performer.

"To become good at football a boy must be constantly playing. At Charterhouse we had an

---

[17] Born, not made (Latin).

excellent institution known as the 'run about'; that is to say, we all used to go to the various football grounds and take either side we likes, and then each boy dribbled as far as he could; kicking the ball was strictly forbidden. This institution, I am sure, is first-rate for the turning out of forwards.

"'Punt about' was another popular form of amusement at school, and very useful it was for teaching one to kick in any position. It consisted of a good many boys kicking footballs to and fro, handling the ball not being allowed."

"By the way, do you think it dangerous for boys to play against men? Or is it the other way about? Perhaps the youngsters know how to upset the men better than the men know how to upset the youngsters!"

"It is a very good thing for boys to play with people better than themselves. This prevents any tendency to selfishness, which, if once acquired, is difficult to shake off; and playing with their superiors also affords boys illustrations of good play, which they can of course imitate and in time acquire."

"How should one practise to become a first-class forward?"

"The qualifications for a forward vary somewhat according to his position. Every forward, however, must have some dribbling powers, and must also be able to pass well. It is essential for an outside forward to be fast, as he gets many opportunities of using his pace; an inside forward need not be so fast, as combination is his chief concern.

"To be able to dribble well is a great advantage, but good passing is of the utmost importance. If a boy is selfish, no matter how good a dribbler he is, he will spoil the team; forwards to be perfect should work like a machine, each being dependent on his companions."

"Now, what of the 'funk', Mr. Smith?—that most estimable of gentleman who would like to pad himself with pillows and mattresses and that sort of thing, and who, whenever one of the opposing side approaches with the ball, clenches his fists and assumes a ferocious let-me-kill you sort of expression, and when the moment for business arrives—quietly ties up his boot-laces."

"There is, I am sorry to say, a good deal of 'funking' at football, and in my opinion it is impossible of cure; a boy if he 'funks' will probably go on 'funking' when he becomes bigger. Oddly enough, the people who 'funk' are generally the ones to get hurt, which fact may perhaps be of use in persuading boys not to adopt such tactics."

"Ah, that reminds me. The public is treated from time to time with a football butcher's bill. We read of awful slaughter and the breaking of thousands of limbs on the field of play; but is football really as dangerous as it is made out to be?"

"I do not thing that the dangers of football are at any time great, and amongst prominent players they are very slight indeed. One hardly ever hears of a bad accident in a good match. The dangers of football arise generally from the inability or rashness of the player. The wild kicking of an unskilful player who doesn't care a nit whether he kicks the ball or an opponent is a great source of danger; but fortunately this sort of player is not often met with. It is the player that creates danger, not the game. On the whole, I believe football to be a safe game. As far as my own experience goes I have never been hurt, and hardly ever seen an accident, and certainly not a very serious one."

"Complaints are sometimes made against the professional footballer, Mr. Smith. The man who makes his bread and cheese out of the game is surely not the double-distilled monster he is occasionally claimed to be?"

"I have been lucky enough to play against nearly all the League teams, and have, therefore, met many professionals. They are a very nice set of men, not only to meet on the football field, but off it. It is quite an exceptional thing to find foul play amongst the leading professional clubs.

When you meet second-class professional the case may be different; but the first-class professional rarely descends to shady tricks, and plays the game in the spirit in which it ought to be played."

"Do you think football is growing more popular every year?"

"As far as I know, football, not only amongst men but also amongst boys, is largely on the increase, and growing more popular every year."

"One more question. Just by way of encouraging youngsters will you tell them what your age was when you played in your first big match?"

"The first really great match in which I played was England v Ireland at Birmingham when I was twenty years old. But before that I had played many times for Old Carthusians, the Corinthians, and Oxford University."

Chums, 14 October 1896

Gilbert Oswald Smith (1872-1943), known as G. O. or "Jo", was the England captain at the time of this interview. An intelligent and selfless centre forward, Smith played at least 20 times for England, scoring 11 goals. An amateur throughout his career, Smith was regarded as one of the greatest players of his time, despite suffering from chronic asthma, which may have coloured his comments on boys who "sham" to avoid football.

Football by the Electric Light

A Football Experiment, 1878

~

THE Sheffield public were last evening introduced to the decided novelty in football—a match
with the assistance of the electric light. The
contest, which took place at Bramhall Lane
Ground between two teams selected by the Sheffield Football Association, was the first ever
played in this country—or anywhere else, we
believe—with the aid of artificial illumination,
especially of that which is derived from the powerful currents of electricity. We had had plenty of
athletic exhibitions by the light of gas—notably
those of recent occurrence at the Agricultural
Hall, London, but little of the kind has been
attempted in the open air. It remained for the
promoters of athletics in Sheffield to lead the
way with a new motor, as they have led the way
in many other directions, by giving the light a
thoroughly public trial. It would have been difficult to select a ground more suitable than Bramhall Lane for a display of the illuminator. Those
who have seen the enclosure under the blaze of a

midsummer sun, with thousands of excited spectators witnessing the performances of Yorkshire's favourite cricketers can hardly possess a complete idea of the black wilderness it presents by night when there is no moon or the heavens are overcast. To walk there is literally like wandering about a bleak moor, for look which way you will scarcely a light can be seen, except it may be from the bedroom windows of an adjoining row of houses. To attempt to illuminate a place like this so that spectators could with ease distinguish the faces and figures of football players at a distance of perhaps two hundred yards appears a somewhat bold proceeding, but the successful manner in which it was done last night shows that Messrs. Tasker in entering upon their undertaking must have been firmly convinced of the power of the illuminator to accomplish a satisfactory result.

So much has been written of late concerning the new light that it is unnecessary for us to enter largely into that matter. Its more general adoption in Paris seems to have given a general fillip to experiments with it in this country. The Avenue de l'Opera has for some time been entirely lighted with it, and its suitability for illuminating railway stations, workshops, and other large establishments is generally admitted. The question remains undecided, however, whether it can be rendered practicable for use by sub-division for domestic purposes. Mr. [Thomas] Edison says it can, for he has just made a most important discovery, by which he states that he can divide the light as freely as gas, and that the illuminator can be manipulated quite as conveniently, at less cost, and with considerably improved effect. Great doubt has been expressed by practical people in England in reference to the ingenious American's latest discovery, but it is evident enough that Mr. Edison has a large number of believers, from the fact that there has been something like a panic in gas shares. We can have nothing to say as to the practicability of sub-dividing the light (as Mr. Edison says "indefinitely") but the spectacle last night at Bramhall Lane conclusively demonstrated that for public purposes the new motor is an undeniable boon, and is certain sooner or later to come into more general use. It may be stated, as bearing out the probability that Mr. Edison has really discovered the process of sub-division, that the machine room of the Times newspaper was lighted by [John] Rapieff's electric light during the printing of last Saturday's issue. It may be that Mr. Edison is somewhat late in the field with his alleged new discovery, but if he has only improved on the contrivances of Rapieff he will have done much to earn the gratitude not only of

the present but of future generations. We now
proceed to give details.

The match was announced to commence at
half-past seven o'clock, and considerably before
than hour the roads to Bramhall Lane were
completely besieged. The wonder was where all
the people came from. There seemed no end to
the ever-coming stream, and the crowd of excited
people outside the gates struggling to pass in at
the turnstiles created a scene of great animation.
The vast enclosure—extensive as it is—appeared
quite crowded, so large was the assembly, and
there must have been a considerable number
who failed to get a fair view of the play, as it was
quite impossible to see over the heads of the
dense masses of humanity, all craning their
necks towards the debateable territory. In
describing the arrangements by which the light
was provided we may state that at each corner of
the ground marked off for the players a wooden
stage was erected some ten yards high for
carrying the lamp and reflector. Behind each
goal was placed a portable engine, each of which
drove two Siemen's dynamo machines—one for
each light. The illuminating power equalled 8000
standard candles, and the cost per hour for each
light was about 3½d. Those who understand
most about the subject are best able to
appreciate the very difficult and critical task

Messrs. Tasker undertook to perform. The engines, being only temporary, required the strictest attention; every light had to be most carefully fixed and protected against the wind and other outside influences. As if endeavouring to rival the artificial illuminator, the lunar orb stood high and bright in the heavens; the atmosphere was pure and pleasant, and it was generally admitted that it would hardly have been possible for either Messrs. Tasker or the Sheffield Football Association to have been favoured with a more suitable evening for the experiment in hand. Everything indeed appeared favourable for the occasion, and after the preliminary experiment on Saturday night it was only to be expected that all arrangements would be carried out by Messrs. Tasker and their assistants. At first the light was certainly too powerful to be looked at with comfort, but Messrs. Tasker soon got it under away, and at once gave convincing proof of their ability to regulate the illuminator. When finally in working order the lights were conducted from the temporary wooden stands fixed to the right and left of each goal, and were elevated thirty feet high. At the four points named a lamp and reflector were fixed, and these, aided by engines behind the goals, formed the means for distributing the current. Everybody seemed highly pleased with the result of the experiment, the light being most brilliant and effective. It may here been stated that the experiment turned out a great financial success, the novelty of the thing drawing together an immense attendance, reaching, in our estimation, nearly twenty thousand people. When everything was in readiness, at 7.30 the distinguishable colours of the two sides were clearly visible, although it was rather difficult to discern the individual movements on the top side of the ground. Whether the lights were fixed to the best advantage is an open question; the general impression was they were slightly too near. Reverting to the match itself, we should state the sides were distinguished by blue and red dresses, Mr. J. C. [Charles] Clegg captaining one team and Mr. W. E. [William] Clegg the other. The Blues won the toss, and selecting the goal nearest the gates, their opponents kicked off, having previously been photographed. The following were the players:—

Reds: F. Stacey, goal; J Housley, J. Hunter, E. Buttery, and F. Hinde, backs; J. C. Clegg (captain), W. Mosforth, A. Woodcock, C. Stratford, H. E. Barber, and G. Anthony, forwards.

Blues: T. Lawson, goal; W. E. Clegg (captain), R. Gregory, T. Buttery, and W. H. Stacey, backs; G. B. Marples, A. Malpas, J. Tomlinson, E. H.

Barber, T. Bishop, and P. Patterson, forwards.

Umpires: W. Skinner, and R. W. Dickinson.

Referee: W. Peirce Dix.

The sides had been so carefully selected that an exciting tussle was expected, and this proved true, for from the very first the play was of the fastest description. One of the first to claim notice was T. Buttery, whose fine returns were duly acknowledged. A fine shot at goal by Hunter being cleverly saved by Lawson, J. C. Clegg then had a corner kick, but the leather was sent in a direction rather wide of the mark. Presently both Mosforth and Woodcock made fine runs, and although they actually failed to lower the Blue's standard, they actually failed to lower the Blue's standard, they kept the leather principally at that end. A rally in front of the Red's goal was the next characteristic feature, but despite the fact that one might with almost certainty have predicted that side's downfall, the ball was eventually got away, only to be twice magnificently returned by W. E. Clegg. Mosforth now drove the leather outside, but after it had been carried to the other end a short delay occurred owing to the spectators crowding on to the boundary line. Resuming Patterson for the Blues made a grand corner kick, but, as previously mentioned, it was difficult to follow the players with anything like certainty. Eventually, after half an hour's play, a goal was registered to the Blues, the successful performer being Tomlinson. Although this success appeared to put the Reds fairly on their mettle, their opponents played up with wonderful determination, and profiting from far superior crossing, made several unsuccessful sorties into the Reds' territory.

On changing ends at half time, the Reds again assumed the command, Mosforth especially distinguishing himself with a most brilliant effort which only just failed to secure the opposing fort. A magnificent throw in by G. Marples was next noticeable, after which all the vigilance of the Reds' goal keeper, F. Stacey, was brought into force to stave off the numerous attacks made by the Blues. Some sharp returns by Gregory and Buttery for their respective sides were followed by grand displays by Patterson and E. Barber, the latter's crossing being really perfection. Hereabouts Anthony made a grand run, and crossing to Mosforth the latter's attempt just went over the bar. Only a few minutes now remained to play, but during this time the Blues managed to secure a second goal, and thus they were returned the victors of a vigorous contest by two goals to nothing.

Speaking of the play, we must say that both sides exhibited wonderful form, although the Blues as a body played better together, and to this may be attributed their success. The contest over, the difficulty was to leave the ground. Such a concourse has never previously been seen at Bramhall Lane, and as the means of exit are not particularly easy, there was quite a scene when the spectators attempted to leave. Great good temper, however, was exhibited by all, and eventually the great crowd cleared away without, as far as we were able to ascertain, the slightest accident.

Sheffield & Rotherham Independent, 15 October 1878

This unusual experiment, arranged in part to promote the local Tasker electrical company, was perhaps not quite as successful as this report suggests. The Manchester Times reported: "Some amusement was caused by the brilliance of the light, which dazzled the players sometimes, and caused some strange blunders." Other sources reported that a horse-drawn waggonette ploughed through the crowd during the match, leaving four people seriously injured. Subsequent experiments in London also failed to impress, and floodlights weren't properly introduced to football for another 70 years.

Calcio, or Football in Italy

Helen Zimmern, 1900

~

CALCIO rudely translated would be simply "kick" in English, and therefore we may infer that it resembles our football. Football in England has come to rival the national game, and it is popularly supposed that it owes its existence to English sportsmen, and was first played in England.

As a matter of fact, the game, in the same manner as many other arts, crafts, and sports, owes its existence to the lands of the south, or rather to the land which before all others gave to the world many idea and notions which, developed and adapted to modern demands, we have appropriated and call ours. The best authorities believe that football in its primitive form was introduced to Britain by the Romans.

It was in Florence, one hundred and sixty years ago, that the last game of Calcio was played on January 19, in honour of the arrival in that city of Francis II of Lorraine with his bride Maria.

This game took place in the ancient piazza of San Gallo, at the edge of the city, and in honour of the valour and skill of the players, and for the delight of the Northern Grand Duke, a triumphal arch was erected to mark the date and the spot. The arch still stands, in truth a monument to the utter lack of taste or artistic knowledge of the those days Florentines; but the game which it was raised to commemorate has passed into memory together with the name of the Grand Duke which it was played to amuse.

An old manuscript which bears the date of 1482 describes almost identically the present-day game of football. It afterwards changed and developed, so that the players increased from eleven to twenty-seven.

Calcio was always considered strictly a gentleman's game, to be played by the nobility, officers, and those specially honoured by the reigning sovereigns, and from the ranks of these only by those who were strong and sound of body. So naively is the ancient book of rules worded that it deserves translation.

The dust-eaten pamphlet says: "Calcio is a game to be played by two sets of young and strong men, without armour or weapons, and is designed for pleasure. It consists in directing a ball of medium size, filled with air and made of leather, over a field, to the honour of the reigning

Grand Duke and the amusement of the gentle
ladies who may grace the performance by their
presence.

"The condition of the men and their physical
capacity must decide the place each player shall
take in the game, for it is true that not all men
are capable to take part in such an heroic effort.
No youth of adolescent age is permitted to play,
because he would be too tender of muscle and too
weak of limb, nor are the senile allowed to enter
the file, for the old are too dry and brittle for
such exercise, and they could not endure the
extreme fatigue and the roughness of handling
which must necessarily be a part of the performance. No servant is allowed to play calcio, no
infamous person, robber, murderer, liar, or trai-
tor, but honourable soldiers, gentlemen and
princes, from the ages of 18 to 45, of strong build,
fair to look upon, and of good temper; for be it
remembered, to the disgrace of mankind, that
there are even princes who will stop to thrust in
hatred their secret enemies, under cover of a
game of chance or a pleasure, when they dare not
attack the in public.

"And above all things the players of calcio
must bear it in mind that their movements are
being watched by ladies, who treasure each
brave act, and who will be more influenced by
the courageous deportment of a player than by a

thousand scented billets."

For two hundred years the game continued in ever-increasing popularity, and when the famous siege of Florence took place, and Michelangelo was defending his beloved birthplace from the overhanging fortress of San Miniato, the starving Florentines each afternoon played their game in all the brilliant attire they could afford, to convince their enemies that they were not cowed by their enforced confinement. Once, during a game, a cannonball came whizzing over the church at the end of the Piazza Santa Croce, cutting away a piece of the cornice, and landing in the centre of the field. It touched no one, and the players calmly continued their game as if nothing had happened. In time, one after another of the brave youths dropped out of the round, and at last they were obliged to abandon their efforts, because, as the record says, "when a man has not tasted bread for twelve days he cannot be very active, and the weight of his stomach is so light that he cannot keep his balance, and his feet career in the air without his consent, which is against the rules of the honoured game of calcio."

The costumes of calcio were of the most expensive and finest stuffs. They consisted of woven silk tights, or *calzone* as they were called. These covered the legs of the players; the feet were incased in soft tanned shoes made all in one piece, without soles, but constructed to fit the foot exactly. The body was covered, first, by a woven silk *maglia* or shirt, and over this was worn a belted tunic of rich stuff, brocade or embroidered linen. Cloth of gold tunics were presented to the players of a famous game of calcio by the Grand Duke Ferdinand de' Medici, and these tunics, or some of them, are still preserved in one of the Florentine museums. The players of the different sides were dressed in different colours, one side taking blue and white, for example, and the other white and red, according to the favourite colours of their respective patrons. The colours were united after the manner of a Pierrot dress, one leg white and one leg blue, the left side of the tunic white and the right side blue, the idea being carried out in the hat and gloves. On the hands were worn skin gauntlets with long pointed wrists, and the caps varied with the seasons, close knitted silk ones in winter and large ventilated helmets in summer.

Calcio of two hundred years ago differs from the modern Association game in that, instead of having eleven men, twenty-seven players were employed. Instead of having five men representing centre, right and left inside forwards, calcio requires five *sconciatori* or defenders; seven *datori* or givers, the first four corresponding to the three half-backs, and the second three to the

CAPTAIN IN ITALIAN FOOTBALL

two full-backs; and fifteen *corridori* or keepers, corresponding to the goalkeeper. These *corridori* are divided into three companies of five each, and protect the goal. They are the only players allowed to touch the ball with their hands; the rest of the players must not touch it with the arm below the elbow. These *corridori* arrange themselves in three positions, the first company keeping itself in front of the goal, and the other two at the sides of the first. There are, in addition to the players described, what are called *trombettieri*, or trumpeters, who sound the beginning and different intervals of play; the *alabardieri* or halberdiers, who are also *corridori*; and the *pallaio* or ball-man, who kicks the

ball from the centre of the field at the commencement of the game. This player takes not
part in the game, except to start the ball or begin
a new round after a foul. He retires from the
field after his kick, and only appears when a new
round takes place. The *pallaio* is dressed in a
combination of the two colours of the contending
players, and serves both sides. In beginning the
play, the two opposing parties start from their
respective tents at the extremes of the field,
march in double file led off by the trumpeters,
the halberdiers bringing up the rear, and meet
the kicker in the centre. The kicker salutes both
sides; then the companies separate, each making
the circuit of the piazza and doing homage to the
royalties present. The members then take their
places, the *pallaio* kicking the first time for the
side which by a toss-up has won the first play.
One other important difference between the two
games is in the hands of the referee, in calcio
there are five men whose duties are to decide the
game. These are a *maestro di campo*, or field-
master, elected by the patron of the game, two
judges elected by him, and a player from each
side, who at intervals meet in the centre of the
ground and compare notes. The season for calcio,
on account of the climate in Italy, was fixed from
January 12, or the first day of Carnival, until
June 24, or St. John's Day, and it is still said in

COMMENCEMENT OF A FOOTBALL MATCH ON
THE PIAZZA DI SANTA CROCE, FLORENCE

the *patois* of Tuscany, if a man does anything out of season or inappropriately, that "he would play calcio in August."

The ancient game has within the past year been revived in Florence in honour of *fêtes* to Paolo Toscanelli and Amerigo Vespucci,[18] and the modern Florentine youths have learned anew the long-forgotten game, copied the antique costumes, and, in the piazza of Santa Croce, which is the historic playing ground, they have performed with all its rites and ceremonies, in honour of Queen Margherita's visit, this game,

---

[18] Florentine mathematician and astronomer (1397-1482) and explorer and cartographer (1454-1512), respectively.

which, in its rich accompaniments, flash and colour, sparkling halberds, sounding trumpets, and brightly caparisoned retinue, cannot but renew its pristine popularity.

The Leisure Hour, March 1900

———————————————

Helen Zimmern (1846-1934) was born in Germany and raised in Britain, where she became an author and translator noted for making European culture accessible to British readers. She moved to Italy in the 1880s, working on the Florence Gazette and the Corriere della Sera. This article was published in The Leisure Hour, an illustrated magazine issued by the Religious Tract Society.

"Football madness was in the air, and it was nearly midnight before enthusiasts could sleep."

Out With a League Team

Henry Leach, 1900

~

"What a jolly fine time you chaps must have, going away with the teams every other week-end!" This was a remark which was often addressed to me during one period of my journalistic career, when it became my humble duty to follow one First Division football team or another up and down the country in its peregrinations for points. Possibly the many who made it would have been less envious if they had experienced some of the discomforts of the business.

For instance, I have yet to learn that it is one of the pleasures of life to be forced to get out of a warm bed at 4.30 A.M. the Saturday before Christmas, to find there is no time to wait for breakfast, and then to trudge two miles through the blackness and a cold drizzling rain to a station where a two hundred miles' journey North is commenced, and to which you will return in the very small hours of the morning.

But, all the same, these little trips are somewhat interesting, especially if one is so young and enthusiastic that the results of League matches are considered of more importance than alliances between foreign Powers. The genus professional footballer, when he goes abroad to meet the enemy, is a distinct study, and as most boys, especially those residing in a "Socker"-infested neighbourhood, have the form of the League clubs weighed up to an ounce, and follow their doings with the closest watchfulness, it occurred to me that they would like to know what takes place as a rule when the teams go away. Few may find out in the ordinary way, for the players' saloon is sacred to all but the players and trainer, committee-men, and the football war correspondents who follow a club faithfully through the glories and disasters of a whole season's campaign.

And let me say here now that the experience has taught me that much injustice is done to the football pros, as a class, by those who know nothing about them. I am no believer in the limited company manner in which Association football is carried on nowadays; but it is wholly unjust to visit the sins of the system upon the men who are the necessary result of it.

From what I have seen of them—and it is very much—they are a very steady and respectable class, and are very probably much better men than they would have been if they had not taken up football as a profession. Regular habits of life are compulsory, and that is a great thing; and I have never known a professional to take any less interest in the game or be any less loyal to his club or solicitous for its welfare than would have been the case if he had been an amateur and did not get well paid for his services. He does not think of his wages when he is on the field, but only of his side and of the victory which he hopes may come of it.

Well, then, the team, with one or two good reserves, is usually selected in good time during the week, and the secretary briefly notifies each man of the arrangements which have been made. His note runs something like this:

"DEAR SIR—You have been selected to play in your usual position in next Saturday's match against Everton; kick-off at 2.30. To be ready for the 8.25 A.M. train at the Midland station, you will please report yourself there at 8.15."

As a matter of fact, that train is not due to leave till 8.35, but the secretary is a good judge of human nature in the matter of catching early trains, and it would never do for a single player to be late. Still, in time the player becomes educated to this little dodge, and looks up the time-table on his own accord, with the result that more than once have I seen an indispensable forward or goal-keeper rushing madly on to the platform, with his arms going about like the sails of a windmill, when the wheels had already begun to move. If the guard sympathises with football, and realises the state of affairs, he will pull the train up, especially if it is a special, as it frequently is; but if his heart is stony those wheels roll on, and there is distress in the players' saloon for a long time, while at the first stopping place execrations are heaped upon the head of that villainous guard.

On one journey we left a player behind in this way, and the match we were going to was one of great importance, for it was generally considered that it would have a lot to do with settling whether our club should rise from the Second Division to the First. There was a reserve in the saloon, but he was not a man to be depended upon; and the state of affairs was distinctly unpleasant.

A brilliant idea occurred to one of the committee-men. Our opponents were Manchester City, and our route to Manchester lay through Derby. At Derby there resided one of our regular first-team players, who had, for some reason or other, been dropped this particular week. What could be simpler than for one of the committee to drop out at Derby, secure this man, and hurry away with him to Manchester by the next train, which would land him there just in time?

But the idea didn't work out very well—at

least, at first it didn't. The official got out and hurried to that man's quarters, only to find that, as he was under the impression he was having a holiday, he was not at home. Away went a telegram to the secretary: "Can't find him," and the secretary became despondent. But the official later on obtained a clue as to the man's whereabouts, and he wired again: "On his track." Up and down Derby he went from one place to another, and at last, only just in time to catch the very last train, which was any good, he was enabled to wire: "Found him. Coming."

But at the Manchester end the coming seemed to be too long delayed. The minutes sped away, and the time for dressing came, and "He cometh not" was the sorrowful reflection of the secretary. The reserve was ordered to turn out, and the players had lined up before a big crowd, when there was a commotion on the rails. A way was made, and an official rushed on to the field and dragged off the unwilling reserve. The eleventh man had arrived, and, of course, if the game had begun with the reserve in the team, it would have had to go on with him, no changing after the start being allowed. The referee wouldn't wait while the eleventh man donned his football toggery, and so our side began with ten men; but soon the other bounded on to the turf, and that day a quite brilliant four-one victory was accomplished.

The same team seemed to be in an even tighter fix than this on another occasion. I may as well say that it was Notts County. We were coming down South with the intention of getting two points out of Arsenal, and the match was of no less importance than the other. The train stopped at Kettering, and two or three of the men got out to stretch their legs. Long railway journeys are very wearisome to trained athletes. Suddenly, without any warning, without any blowing of the guard's whistle, the train began to move on. The secretary shouted out, and the players on the platform made a rush for the carriage-door, and, as it seemed, all got safely inside and congratulated themselves on being so close at hand. From a large party it is not difficult to miss one man, and we had gone some little distance before a most hideous fact dawned upon us, which threatened to bring about an immediate and universal greying of hair. [George] Toone, the goal-keeper, many times International, whose place really could not be filled, was missing! The time-table was appealed to in vain for consolation. There was no other train from Kettering which could land him in London in time.

A council of war was held, and the inevitable was accepted with all the grace possible under the circumstances. A rearrangement of the team was decided upon, and a half-back was ordered to go between the sticks. The outlook was gloomy, and it was by no means a safe proceeding to attempt to open up any conversation with the secretary, even on such an innocent subject as the weather.

On reaching King's Cross the party filed across the road to a restaurant, where orders were given for steaks for fourteen. We hadn't been sat down more than ten minutes waiting for those steaks to cook, when, in a manner peculiar to him, but which was certainly very tantalising in these times, Toone quietly walked in and sat down amongst us as if nothing had happened. Helped by a lot of luck, he had made a very good best of a very bad job. When he found that the train had left him at Kettering, he naturally cast his eyes about him for another, and there on the other side of the line he saw one waiting to go out. It was a train which was behind its time, and should have been on the other. It was promptly boarded, and that is why an extra steak had to be ordered at King's Cross, and also, very likely, it was the reason why Woolwich Arsenal were beaten, for Toone, as if to make up for his morning's faults, played a very great game that afternoon.

But now let me say something about what

goes on in the saloon in a general way, and about the arrangements which are made for the comfort and well-being of the party.

Of course the saloon is always engaged, no matter whether the journey to be made is short or long. It is a detail that in the case of a party of such dimensions the railway company makes no extra charge for it. It is necessary that all the men should be together, and under the eye of the trainer and the secretary, who also acts as manager. The latter gets all the tickets (fare and a-quarter for the double journey) and distributes them, gratuitously of course, when the train is in motion. Each man usually has his bag with him; but, as a rule, the trainer, who always accompanies the team, is largely responsible for shirts and knickers, and keeps them all in his own hamper. Another very important matter to which he attends is the commissariat, for in a large number of cases it is necessary to lunch in the train. Therefore the hamper is laden with goodly things—not fancy things, but good gig joints of roast beef, and loaves of bread, with a few pots of pickles, which have to be consumed very sparingly.

Nobody has such an appetite as your well-trained footballer, and about midday, very fidgety, and tired of doing nothing, his thoughts turn towards eating and fitting himself bodily for the fray before him.

Not till the trainer will it, however, is his hunger to be appeased; but by-and-by this autocrat disappears into the little ante-chamber at the end of the saloon, a clatter of knives and forks is heard, and presently he emerges with a pile of crockery, which he follows up with the big lumps of beef, the loaves of bread, and all the other comestibles which in his wisdom he has provided for his crew. The secretary, or whoever is most skilful with the carvers, promptly commences to deal out the grub, and by the time he gets to No. 7, No. 1 is clamouring for more!

Eventually, however, the hunger of all is appeased, and then, with a happy contentment and an optimism which is the normal result of a full stomach, the men discuss the coming encounter and the number of goals they will probably win by.

At best, however, these outward railway journeys are weary affairs, for there is so much anxiety as to what is going to happen. Coming home, either victorious or beaten, is ever so much easier. The saloon is strewn with the morning papers, all invariably open at the football page, on which is very likely to be printed the names of the opposing team. This naturally becomes the subject of keen discussion, and it is a matter for all-round congratulation if from some cause or other the rivals are a little below strength.

The grown footballer is not infrequently a smoker, but on no account is he allowed to smoke in the saloon on the journey out. This rule is most strictly enforced, not so much perhaps on account of the injury it would do to the smoker himself, as on account of the contamination of the atmosphere which would ensue, for it is one of the first principles of the trainer that his mean must breathe pure air. Now and again, however, you see a player get up and evince some curiosity as to what is in that little ante-chamber afore-said. He looks about for a moment, and then, as if by accident, the door quietly closes. A couple of minutes later another player follows him, and as the door opens you get a sniff of tobacco which tells a tale of guilt, and the little game is promptly stopped. No great harm, however, is done.

~

Things are usually so arranged that on the team's arrival at its destination there is but little time cut to waste, for nothing so much depresses the football player away from home, and dis-counts his side's chances of victory, as an aimless idling about for an hour or two before the match.

He knows he is in a hostile country, and that

it would be foolish to expect either the admiration or the respect to which he is treated when he is on his own pitch. Instead of that, these foreign urchins make it their business to discover at the earliest possible moment all the weak points in his physique and the peculiarities of feature, and to communicate the results of their researches to each other in stage asides, which are audible to all, and most of all to the man criticised. An argument arises also as to the precise number of goals by which the home side will beat their visitors. As a rule the consensus of opinion inclines to six, but sometimes double figures are favoured.

Some very big boys, who ought to know better, but don't, occasionally follow the example of the youngsters in these matters; and, though it is all very wise and well to say that no man with any common-sense would take notice of such folly, it all adds to that feeling of sojourning in a strange land the ultimate result of which is a lost match.

Everybody knows that a good team stands more chance of winning at home than it does away, and I should say, speaking without the book, that the average League eleven—the "average" is important here—wins three matches at home for every one on foreign soil. Why? Certainly not because it is more familiar with its own ground than any other. Many people fancy this is the reason, but every League player whom I have sounded on the question denies it. And I agree with them. Except in such cases as Newcastle United, the ground of which the ancient Britons might have thought good for football, but which the modern artist always dreams of in his worst nightmares, the playing patch of one League club is so like that of another that a forward pegging away at top speed scarcely ever notices any difference. Now and again, on a small ground, when he does look up, he is crossing the goal line just when he begins to think it is time to put in a long shot, but that is all. It is the morning's anxiety, the restlessness, and the lack of public sympathy which cause a visiting team to be beaten so often—and particularly the anxiety, because in the case of League clubs fighting for position everything depends upon the away matches.

In speculating upon the possible and probable results of its matches at the commencement of the season a club always takes it for granted that it is going to win its home matches. If it cannot do this it stands a poor chance away, and it might as well "put its shutters up" at once. An observation I have made which bears out what I have said is to the effect that, whether a team pulls the game out of the fire or not, it nearly always plays better in the second half away from home than it does in the first. So much for that point.

The footballer abroad has many anxious thoughts for those at home, as he plainly shows when he hurries up to a friend who has come with them, just before going on the field, and hands him a big batch of addresses telegram forms, with the humble request that he will send half away at half-time with the score, and the other at the finish.

Sometimes, if there are parents at home who look upon football as only less dangerous than standing with one's back to the muzzle of a hostile Maxim gun, a further request is also made that in the last telegram there shall be an indication that the sender's neck, arms and legs are still intact—in short, that all is well.

I particularly remember the case of a friend of mine, who was nonetheless playing, as amateurs sometimes do, in the ranks of a team which was otherwise wholly professional. A very good half-back he was, too, and he loved the game intensely. The club for which he played was located some thirty or forty miles away from his home, so that this journey had to be made for all home matches, and it was an extra when his side had to go away. The "governor" was very sorely set against this footballing, and it was grudgingly that he waived his scruples at this point. Consequently, I received standing instructions from my friend always to send a telegram home at close with the result, and the words "All well". The said standing instruction was given to me because, as he said, he himself might forget sometimes, and it was nice to have somebody to depend upon—and blame. He said that if a match began at three o'clock, the "governor" at home spent the time between half-past four and five in walking to and fro uneasily between the post-office and his home, and it was with a great sense of relief that the brown envelope was at length delivered to him.

Woe was me! In an evil hour one Saturday afternoon, having a lot of extra matter to put upon the wires, I forgot the telegram to the dad, and the reproaches cast upon me a week later almost made me quiver with repentance.

But I remember at least one occasion on which I had to send a sorrowful message to a player's home, though not to this player's home. It was from one of the most exciting Cup ties I have seen. Aston Villa were then at the head of the League, and without doubt a team of extraordinary brilliance. It is the usual thing for those who are learned in football history to say that the Preston North End team from 1887 to 1889 was the finest that ever stepped on to a field; that it was the forwards' pleasure to take the ball from one goal to another, passing it from one foot to the next, without ever letting it touch the ground; and so on. Certainly, I grant that a team containing such men as N. J. Ross, a prince of backs, R. Holmes, David Russell, John Goodall, Drummond, and a few of the others of such calibre, was necessarily a fine one; but I doubt, if it could have been pitted against the Aston Villa eleven of two or three years ago, whether it could have achieved victory. Preston North End taught us what combination could be, and, as the only club of that time who attained anything near perfection, they naturally asserted a great superiority over their rivals, and this superiority made us think at the time that they were a far more brilliant team than they really were. Aston Villa asserted the same superiority over teams which were ever so much stronger than the opponents of the North Enders, and in a day when combination and the science of football generally was made the closest study of by all clubs, high and low, and when the game had developed amazingly from what it was in the eighties, they yet toyed with most of the elevens pitted against them as if they were children.

This is a digression. The point I want to bring out is the strength of the Birmingham men this particular year, and the utter hopelessness, as it seemed, of the task set Notts County when they were drawn against them in the first round of the English Cup competition. To make things worse, the match was to be played at the Villa ground. Notts were then at the head of the second division, and, therefore, nominally the seventeenth best club in the country. Actually I should say that they were about the fourth or fifth just then. They went into very special training for this match; but I cannot think that anyone connected with the club thought they had the remotest chance of winning. But they came very near it. The men were in the pink of condition and played beautifully, and very early on in the game a free kick taken by a full back was placed in the right spot to an inch, and was headed through the Villa goal. With a point in hand they played desperately, and, though their famous opponents realised now that they had their work cut out and bent themselves to it with a will, they could make no headway. They were penned in their own half, and as often as they tried to get away the Notts halves vetoed their attempts. Conspicuous among these halves was Charlie Bramley, who had aforetime helped Notts to the pinnacle of fame, being one of the team that won the Cup. He was playing as steadily as a rock. Out from the Villa pack came the famous Crabtree, with the ball at his toes. Bramley rushed to meet him. Two legs shot towards each other at the same moment, and the next one Bramley lay on the ground with a compound fracture of the leg! I was standing near the touch line at the time, about thirty yards away, and the crack smote my ears like the falling of a stack of timber. It rang out all over the ground. Notts' chances had gone!

The affair, of course, was purely accidental, and there was not a particle of roughness in the play which brought it about. Crabtree is a thorough gentleman-professional on the field, and he was dreadfully cut up about it. A stretcher was brought into the arena. Bramley was laid upon it, and a surgeon temporarily bound up the broken limb. He bore himself bravely, and was in no spirit of bravado that he asked for a cigarette, and, obtaining it, proceeded to smoke it whilst still lying there! I asked him if there was anything he would like me to do for him. Yes, there was just one thing; would I wire his father to say that, though his leg was broken, he was all right? Then they carried him to a Birmingham hospital, where he lay for over a month. A broken leg is bad enough for anybody; but it is perhaps worse for a professional footballer not in the first blush of youth than to anybody else.

From that moment Bramley was dead to first-class football. Those who think there is no more sportsmanlike chivalry left in football may reflect upon the fact that Aston Villa, then the greatest possible attraction to the football world, and a team run at tremendous expense, promptly offered to play their full team in a match, either at Birmingham or Nottingham, for Bramley's benefit, free of any charge whatsoever. Trent Bridge was chosen, and a substantial cheque for the beneficiary was the result.

As for this Cup tie, the Villa won, but only just; they soon equalised; and once looked as if they would never get the winning goal. The ghost of Bramley seemed to lead on those ten men of Notts, and it was only at the very finish that the Villa won from a corner. It was the hardest match they had, though they went right through the competition and won the Cup. Twenty thousand people watched it, of whom sixteen thousand were supporters of the Birmingham men; but so much was sympathy with the visitors after their loss of Bramley, that I believe at the finish the crowd was just a trifle disappointed that its own side had won.

~

League teams inevitably play two games the same day. One is fought on the field, and another commences in the dressing-room immediately afterwards.

A separate dressing-room is, of course, provided on every ground for each of the teams, and the scene inside during the half-hour following the blowing of the "Time" whistle is one full of animation, no matter whether victory or defeat has attended the efforts of the men. The only difference this makes is the point of view from which each man discusses—first, the referee; second, his colleagues; and third, the enemy.

If the result is a win, all are as good as good can be; and while the trainer, beaming with satisfaction, rubs away at the legs of the centre-forward, that worthy shouts across to a full-back who is scraping the mud from his face, to compliment him on an exceedingly neat piece of work, whereby single-handed he stopped a mad rush of the whole of the opposing forward line.

The full-back realises that the proper thing to do under the circumstances is to express to the company his admiration for the shot with which the centre-forward scored the winning goal, which was absolutely the very finest he had ever seen in his life. And so the merry prattle goes on, till all have been bathed and rubbed and tidied up, so that they are fit to go out into the outside world again.

All the timidity with which they moved amongst that throng of strangers before the battle-blast was blown has vanished now. They walk abroad through the streets of the enemy with a proud consciousness of superiority, and pretend not to hear the remarks of the little boys, who have come to the conclusion that they are a much better lot than they at first supposed. Under such happy circumstances as these it is the wont of the players of a League team to keep together, and the officials, too, form part of the company which wends its way to the big hotel of the place, where a very high tea is ordered. At each end of the table steams rises from large plates of chops and steaks, and during the meal yet a third game is played.

The outside right, fully conscious that he did all that human man could do, but craftily fishing for a compliment, declares that he blames himself severely for not scoring when he received that lovely pass from Jones. There is a chorus of dissent, one and all declaring that the outside right played the best game of his life. He blushingly protests, but all to no purpose; and then the goalkeeper recounts how he saved four hot shots in thirty seconds!

It is so different in defeat. Each man thinks there were ten bad players in the team, and one good one; but the conversation is not so free. It is deemed wisest to maintain an attitude of sullen reserve to everybody. The trainer is most talkative, and expresses his opinions very bluntly. He knew what was going to happen—in fact he told all his friends some days before that if they got off with a four-goal defeat they would be lucky! With a very angry candour he impresses upon each man, as his turn for rubbing comes, the necessity of an immediate reformation if he wishes to keep his place in the team, and declares moreover that if he, the trainer, had his way, he would never play again. What did he tell him on Monday? How were his orders disobeyed on Tuesday? And where was that wretched player on Wednesday when the others were at practice? There is no great gathering in the hotel now. The secretary gives each man half-a-crown to go and get his tea "somewhere", and in couples they slink out, and are seen no more till train time!

On the journey home events are discussed in a more philosophic manner. Officials do not reproach the men for the defeat. Rather do they seek to restore fallen spirits, with here a "Can't be helped," and there a "Never mind, lads— better luck next time."

If it is a long journey, a few of the men, tired out with anxiety and severe play, drop off into a slumber, and the remainder converse in low tones. Not surprising can it be that these healthy athletes can fall to sleep in the train by nine o'clock in the evening.

Once we had to go to a League match at New-castle-upon-Tyne, and the committee decided that we should start the same morning and not travel overnight. And a miserable morning it was, too, when we turned out at about four o'clock. I think it was after one when we got to our stopping place in the North. A very early kick-off had been arranged, and there was only just time to get to the ground; and as soon as the match was over we had to bolt for the train again, and landed home at about four in the morning. That was rather stiff for twenty-four hours, yet nobody minded, for a draw was effected, and a point secured which had hardly been expected.

When the expense in such matters is not considered by the big clubs, it may seem a trifle strange to some of you that the travelling should not have been done the day before, so that the men would be fresh and vigorous on the day of the encounter. Surely it would seem that their chances of victory were very much discounted by that dreadful ride on that cold winter's morning, what time their opponents were sleeping peacefully in their beds in Newcastle.

Yes; but just then the committee were afflicted to a theory. It so happened that the preceding match away from home was at Blackpool, and in view of certain aspirations it was regarded as highly desirable that a win should be booked on that occasion. Consequently, the team was despatched at midday on Friday, arrived at the Lancashire watering-place early in the evening, and after a good meal took a pleasant walk along the front. They turned in early, and the order "Lights out" at ten o'clock was implicitly obeyed. In the morning all were fresh as daisies; but in the afternoon they lost! It was a bitter pill to swallow. Various theories were propounded for the defeat, but the one most generally favoured by the committee was that the sleeping in strange beds had done it. It seemed to me a rather whimsical theory; but the players associated themselves with it at once, principally, I suspected, because it took all the blame from their own shoulders. That was why the next big journey was commenced when the rest of the world was asleep.

For joy and happiness on the part of the men and officials after a great match, two home-goings stand out in my mind before all others.

The first was in the initial round of the English Cup competition a few years ago, and we were drawn to play against Wolverhampton Wanderers away from home. The chances of pulling it off seemed very small indeed. The Wanderers were a much stronger team than ours then; they had the immense advantage of playing at home; the form of our men was unusually poor; and, worst of all, there was no money in the club till to put them through a special course of training. The simple fact of the matter was that the club was in very low water, and it was realised that if it was to continue its existence something would have to be done. For "something" could be substituted "win or draw at Wolverhampton", which would mean half-share in another Cup-tie "gate", always big ones. Consequently, a public fund was raised, and after some difficulty enough money was scraped together to provide the players with special training at a quiet and healthy country place.

It made a wonderful difference to them, and they seemed as fit as fiddles when they turned out at Wolverhampton. The first half of the game, however, went dead against them, and all chance of averting defeat seemed to have vanished when half-time arrived and the score was 2-0 in favour of the Wolverhampton men. Then, however, the training came in. Our men stayed right up to the finish—improved, in fact, as the time went on—whilst the other side fell to pieces. A goal came, and then the equaliser, but though we pressed desperately towards the close, and were very unlucky, no winning point could be secured. The match had, therefore, to be re-played on the following Wednesday.

What a journey home it was that night! Some thousand followers of the club had gone to see the match, and took with them flags of the colours of the club, for use in case the hoped result should come off. Those flags waved in the breeze outside the carriage windows all the way back, and at every stopping-place they were frantically shaken, to the accompaniment of vigorous cheering, that all the world might know there was life in the old dog yet.

Inside the players' saloon, the scene was pathetic. The achievement was too much to talk about, and most of the players were occupied in building aerial castles, and speculating upon what they would do with the Cup when they got it.

Two players would discuss an incident of the game in which they were jointly concerned; there would be expressions of mutual admiration, and then a soft lingering shake of the hands.

Arrived home, a roaring welcome was accorded them, and for ninety-six hours the cup of contentment was full. There was a melancholy sequel. On the following Wednesday the Wanderers came for the replayed match, and won by four goals to three!

One time, however—and this is the other happy-home-going I alluded to—there was no after sorrow to mar the memory of the day. The victory, too, was of much more consequence than the other would have been—in fact, it was the consummation of a whole season's patient work, and the realisation of a three-years' dream.

Our team, having got to the top of the Second Division of the League, had earned its right to play against the bottom clubs of the First Division in the test-matches, and if it proved successful in them it would go up, at the expense of one of the seniors. There were four of the test-matches, and things so eventuated that everything depended upon the last one.

We had to visit Burnley, and either draw or win; and, since Burnley had previously drawn with us at home, our prospects of going up into the First Division looked anything but rosy at this stage. The anxiety on the outward journey was intense, and it was a relief to all when, early on this April evening, the game began.

It was fast and furious from start to finish. For excitement there has never been anything like these test-matches; often they have meant life or death to the clubs concerned. Our men were promised 10/. each extra if they did what was wanted, and right well they earned it. A goal was scored by them at an early stage of the game, and, by magnificent defensive play, they retained this lead to the finish, winning by the narrowest of margins. But it was enough; the promotion had been secured, and there was joy in the camp.

The Burnley people were dismayed! They had counted upon an easy win for their pets, but they had lost; and now they would have to go down. It was horrible. In their anger all kinds of calumnies about our players were spread, and threats of reports to the Association about breaches of rules were freely made use of. But, to their credit, be it said that their sportsmanlike instinct soon reasserted itself, and when we left Burnley station there were not a few there to give us a cheer—much as it cost them—and to congratulate us on a fine performance.

That was a journey home! Three or four years before, the club had lost its position among the elect just as Burnley had done that day. Now the football paradise had been regained. Many of the team belonged to it in its former days as one of the First League, and on these the effect was greatest. They could not speak. They could only smile consent when you spoke to them of all the glory of the day. The International goalkeeper, hardened against emotion by many seasons' severe campaigns, declared himself to be happy at last; and the captain, David Calderhead, one of the best captains who ever stepped on to a field, echoed that sentiment.

At such times the hours of homeward

travelling drag wearily, for the men and officials yearn for the plaudits of those at home, who they know will be at the station to welcome them. As home is neared all become restive, and the railway companies are blamed because the carriage-windows are not wide enough for six great bodies to lean through at once.

At last the whistle shrieks, you hear the break put on, the train slackens speed, and finally, amidst deafening cheers, runs into the station and finishes its day's work, for it is a special. This particular time it was long past midnight— somewhere about two o'clock, I think—when we got it; but there was a crowd of many hundreds of people on the platform waiting for us, and their cheers and waving of flags lasted many minutes. The players were carried away on shoulders, and outside were mounted on trucks and asked for speeches. Football madness was in the air, and it was nearly midnight before enthusiasts could sleep.

And now, I will draw down again the veil which I raised to show something of the ways and thoughts and feelings of the men who constitute a great League club of to-day. I could write many more of such columns; but I think I have already shown that the business is not so black as it is painted, and that, even though a football player be paid for his services, he may still remain a gentleman and a sportsman. Just as there are black sheep in every fold, there are professional football players here and there who do the game no credit. But for the most part, as those who knew them best will agree, they are a respectable set of fellows, and, as I said at the beginning, are in all probability better men than they would be if they did not play the game they love so well, and be paid for doing so.

Chums, 10 March 1900

Henry Leach (b. 1874) began his career as a local football reporter, before being appointed editor of the Nottingham Evening News while still in his early 20s. In 1898 he moved to London to write about sport for various publications including boys' weekly Chums. He went on to become a leading writer on golf, and the editor of Golf Illustrated. Leach also conducted the interview with Frank Brettell included in this collection.

Victorian Football Timeline

~

1840 – Cambridge Rules created.

1857 – Sheffield FC formed.

1858 – Sheffield Rules created.

1862 – Notts County FC formed.

1863 – Football Association formed.
       Laws of the Game created.

1864 – First association football match.

1871 – FA Cup tournament created.

1872 – First official international match.

1873 – Scottish Football Association formed.

1876 – Football Association of Wales formed.

1878 – Newton Heath FC formed.
       West Bromwich Albion formed.

1880 – Preston North End formed.
       Irish Football Association formed.

1882 – Tottenham Hotspur FC formed.

1884 – British Home Championship created.

1885 – Professionalism in football legalised.

1888 – The Football League formed.

1889 – Northern League formed.

1891 – Scottish Football League formed.

1894 – Southern Football League formed.

1900 – Great Britain wins Olympic football gold.

Bibliography

~

Newspapers and periodicals:

Every Boy's Magazine, February 1862
Bell's Life in London, 31 October 1863
Bell's Life in London, 16 January 1864
Bell's Life in London, 7 December 1872
The Graphic, December 1872
Sheffield &Rotherham Independent, 15 Oct 1878
Newcastle Weekly Courant, 21 October 1887
Pall Mall Gazette, 25 February 1888
Pall Mall Gazette, 24 March 1888
Pall Mall Gazette, 26 March 1888
Daily News, 15 October 1892
The Globe, December 1892
Cassell's Saturday Journal, December 1892
Manchester Times, 2 & 5 March 1894
The Dart, 9 March 1894
Sydney Mail, 14 & 21 April 1894
Chums, 14 October 1896
Manchester Times, 2 September 1898
Chums, 19 October 1898
Chums, 10 March 1900
The Leisure Hour, March 1900

Books:

Alcock, C. W., *The Football Annual*, 1869

Scottish Football Association Annual, 1880

Bone, David Drummond, *Scottish Football Reminiscences and Sketches*, John Menzies, 1890

Shearman, Montague, *Athletics and Football*, Longmans, Green & Co, 1894 (4th Edition)

About the Editor

~

Paul Brown is a writer and editor from the North East of England. He has written about football for publications including The Guardian, FourFourTwo, When Saturday Comes and Loaded. His football books include Balls: Tales from Football's Nether Regions, and Unofficial Football World Champions. He has a website at www.stuffbypaulbrown.com and can be found on Twitter as @paulbrownUK.

More

~

A second volume of Goal-Post will include:
C. B. Fry on the merits, or otherwise, of football.
How to form a football club by T. Murray-Forde.
Woolwich Arsenal's James Jackson interviewed.
Alfred Davis on the Football Annuals.
The first final: Wanderers v Royal Engineers.
Letters from a Lover of Football.
And much more.

For more information and extra content visit:

www.victorianfootball.co.uk

Lightning Source UK Ltd.
Milton Keynes UK
UKOW041814171012

200755UK00003B/6/P